D1353383

Why Does My Dog Do That?
Because…
it's A DOG!

By

Robin Glover

and

Caroline Spencer

Why Does My Dog Do That? Because...it's A DOG!
By Robin Glover and Caroline Spencer
www.puredoglisteners.com

ISBN: 978-0-9567639-0-7

This book is published by Robin Glover and Caroline Spencer in conjunction with Writersworld Ltd. and is available to order from most book shops and internet book retailers throughout the United Kingdom.

Edited by Brian Stanton

Cover Design by Charles Leveroni

Cartoon illustrations by Caroline Spencer

Printed and bound by
www.printondemand-worldwide.com

www.writersworld.co.uk
Writersworld Ltd., 2 Bear Close, Woodstock, Oxfordshire, OX20 1JX, United Kingdom

The text pages of this book are produced via an independent certification process that ensures the trees from which the paper is produced come from well managed sources that exclude the risk of using illegally logged timber while leaving options to use recycled paper as well.

This book is dedicated to the loving memory of

Caroline's dear father, Ben Bezance,

an extraordinary man.

Making behavioural issues a thing of the past.

Vet recommended.

CONTENTS

Acknowledgements

We would like to thank Guy Wolverson BVSc (Hons) MRCVS for his support and belief, Liz Murphy for her expert proof reading, Leslie Harris (APDL) for her brilliant poems.

To our ever-patient families who have had to put up with us being glued to our computers for the last eighteen months - thank you for your patience.

Very importantly, our appreciation to our ever growing gang of PURE Dog Listeners throughout the United Kingdom and across the world, whose support and loyalty is very humbling.

To the Yellowstone Wolves and the Dingoes in Australia, and not forgetting all our dogs, past and present, who have taught us so much and continue to do so.

Introduction

Most dog owners don't want Lassie, Rin Tin Tin or Wonder Dog: they want a friend, a dog that walks nicely on the lead, that comes back when called, is non-aggressive and is generally well behaved. One that will be accepted anywhere they go and will not embarrass them. In short, a dog they can enjoy.

People all over the world are constantly studying different species of animals. Whatever the species they are all studied in their natural environment so the humans present can see how they interact with each other both in groups and as individuals - how they work within the great scheme of things to survive. Generally we now understand that to research wild animals and fully understand them it is best to see them as nature intended without the interference of man. Gone, happily, are the cruel zoos of yesteryear where animals were confined in small barred cells like criminals, with no account of their size or basic needs as dictated by nature. Most zoos now will at least attempt to replicate a natural environment for their captive animals. Although it's not ideal to confine animals, it is a sad truth that some species would not be with us today if it were not for the intervention of some of the more forward-looking zoos.

Not only are zoos 'going back to nature' but so are farmers and home food producers. We let chickens in the domestic environment be just that, chickens, and gradually battery hens are going out of favour. The same applies to other domestic and farm animals…we work with their nature not against it. Shoppers are getting more demanding in wanting to know where their Sunday joint came from and if it was ethically produced or free range. Even our vegetables are more and more organic.

It's a different story though when it comes to the domestic dog, man's best friend. We expect them to take orders from us, do as we tell them when we tell them and have little or no empathy for their natural instincts. We mean well but we humanise them and expect them to understand our every word.

When you see animals in the wild they are calm and relaxed, unless of course they are threatened by danger or on the hunt. Even here there is method and a hierarchy in place to deal with this in a logical way. Look at wildlife films of wolves and wild dogs: they work as a team, they all know their place in the pack and how they fit in.

Our modern day dog's ancestor is the wolf. They share almost identical DNA as well as behaviours so it is a logical thing to look to these animals for guidance on how they communicate and work as a team.

Within our human family we have to set boundaries, it is the same within a pack of dogs, and remember, the term 'pack' is a word devised by humans to describe a family of dogs or wolves, as a pride describes a family of lions. Within all these families, if there were no rules or boundaries then the group would not function at top level and therefore their survival would be compromised. We are closely related to the chimpanzee - sharing 98% of genes, they are our closest living relatives and have been shown to be very similar to humans in appearance and social behaviours. Dogs are very closely related to the wolf - sharing 99.6% of DNA, so it only seems sensible to study wolves and all other canines including the domestic dog to truly understand their communication skills, their social behaviours and society.

(Robin)
Like many people I've had dogs from childhood. I've always loved them and cared for them to the best of my ability. Looking back now I realise that I didn't really understand them, although of course, I thought I did. Don't we all?

On reaching adulthood I joined the Metropolitan Police, first patrolling the streets of Soho before moving to the Special Patrol Group at Scotland Yard. It was at this stage, in the middle of a terrorist bombing campaign in 1973, that I was inspired by a conversation with a bomb dog handler who had read a research paper about the close wolf/domestic dog link. He said that he wasn't convinced about everything in the paper but that there was a huge amount of evidence to support the conclusions. He certainly grabbed my attention. As a result I went on to read and watch anything and everything I could find on the subject such as 'Dog Watching' by Desmond Morris. From this grew a fascination for the natural behaviour and a search for knowledge on how to tap into the dog's thinking.

I transferred from London to Hampshire and successfully applied to join the Dog Section. At first I trained the traditional Police way, which is positive and involves a lot of play. It can however be a little rigid. I was blessed with an open-minded boss who allowed me to implement my research into every aspect of my operational work, moving away from the established training regimes. The increase in success rates on searches, tracks and other deployments was remarkable. This led to a Chief Constable's Commendation in 1988. The citation read *Commended for consistent good work, tenacity and intelligent application of his Police Dog 'Acco' during 1988.* As the human side of the partnership I of course took all the credit but all I had really done was allow Acco to be a dog and show what great animals dogs are and how much untapped potential they have.

On retirement from the Police Service I was privileged to be able to continue to help dogs and their owners reach a better understanding and make life a lot less stressful for both. I met and worked with other like-minded individuals to 'mend dogs'. One of these, with whom I went on to found PURE Dog Listeners, is Caroline Spencer.

(Caroline)
I have had dogs all my life, growing up with a gorgeous Golden Retriever who's only foible was to chase rabbits, steal my teddies from my bed once I'd

gone to school, then take them to her own and look after them until my return.

Whilst working as a school nurse I purchased my first puppy, a black Labrador called Harvey. He was a super boy but we did tend to go on two separate walks, starting off together and then rejoining at the end, not ideal it has to be said.

I was introduced to working dog training and was impressed to see a lady with six dogs at heel walking across a field without any leads. I wanted to be able to do that. I worked with my dog under the watchful eye of various people and was a little alarmed at some of the aggressive training methods, like yanking a dog on the lead to make it heel. I'm embarrassed to say I followed suit.

As time went on I was invited to do demonstrations at country shows with my dogs. I distinctly remember my first one, microphone in hand with adrenaline running high and a couple of hundred spectators followed shortly by the microphone going down and my little cocker spaniel trotting off to the nearest little girl for a cuddle. Glitches over, the demonstration went really well and I went on to do many more over a two year period.

I then got married and did the baby thing and it was then I started to think that maybe there was a kinder more holistic approach to dog training. We bring our children up in a kind caring way to guide them through the rights and wrongs: I've never smacked my children and even though I say so

5

myself they are pretty lovely kids.

So why do we have to bribe, intimidate and demand obedience from our dogs? Why not look deeper into the dog and translate what they are telling us so we can guide them to the rights and away from the wrongs, so we work in harmony with their natural language and instincts. I watched my dogs interact with each other and listened to what they were communicating to each other. There was a leader in my pack and he never intimidated - they followed him because a certain trust existed between them.

I built on this and tried to emulate what he was doing and consolidated my own study by reading books written by John Fisher and Desmond Morris and watched countless videos on wolves. I attended a course on Dog Listening and it helped to re-enforce what I'd been doing.

Dog listening is not only about communicating with dogs but with people and my work as a nurse has most definitely helped me in a variety of ways.

I have been on radio a couple of times, which was pretty scary at first. But talk about what I love and you can't stop me!

I've been working professionally as a dog listener for seven years now: can't really call it work as I love it so much.

(Both)

Jointly, our quest has included watching wolves in Yellowstone and dingoes in Australia. Back in the UK we've observed and in some cases been involved with the training of working dogs of all types: police dogs, guide and assistance dogs, gun dogs, search and rescue dogs, customs and military dogs. A visit to a hunt kennel to see the pack hierarchy and the interaction within the 'den' environment was also a valuable learning experience. Put that together with the information we get from our own and clients' pet dogs and you'll see that we have a huge pool of resources to draw on. We've progressed to where we are today through determination, driven on by our hopes of making the world a better place for our dogs and the humans in their lives. We never stop learning.

The human race began domesticating wolves thousands of years ago. Recent studies in Russia have revealed how this was probably done. They used the silver fox, an animal famed for its aggressive temperament, and picked the calmer and more placid pups. Within three generations they found they were producing foxes that were able to interact with humans. Even more amazing was the fact that not only had they produced a gentler personality but that physical changes were happening too, both in colour and general appearance - some animals having floppy ears for instance. This almost certainly happened with the wolf as the brighter ones realised that there was a food source available if they hung around human settlements. Both sides of the partnership benefited:

the wolves through food and the humans by early warning and protection and subsequently by working together when hunting. As the changes in the wolves' colours and body shape occurred naturally, we humans would no doubt have hurried things along by encouraging the changes we liked. As a result vastly different looks appeared, culminating in the huge variety of domestic dogs we have today.

So in essence we have different looks and kinder (as perceived by humans) personalities, but the brain make-up and communication are the same. Domestic dogs have the capacity to understand us to a certain extent - more so than even chimps which are thought to be our closest relatives - but we must be aware that within each breed and litter there are many personalities just as there are in the human family. This is what we work with: individual personalities. As with teaching anyone, how easily the student will learn depends largely on personality and intelligence. If the dog thinks the teacher is not up to the job then learning will be limited.

When we talk of 'traditional' trainers, the word 'traditional' is rather a misnomer: 'Traditional' as in "We've always done it that way." But we're communicating with a different species, the canine, and they've never 'Done it that way.' They've got their own way of doing things that has served them very well for thousands of years. That's the way we as PURE Dog Listeners do it because it works and the light comes on in the dogs eyes as they make a connection with us and their owners, so perhaps it is the PURE Dog Listener who is really the traditionalist.

If the pupil will not learn the way we teach,
then we will teach the way the pupil will learn.

Ignacio Estrada

To keep it as close as we can to natural canine communication we make our interaction with the dog replicate its own behaviour in the wild as closely as possible, in all areas. For that reason we steer clear of gadgets. We do use collars and leads because the law requires us to. Sometimes a harness can be a useful replacement for the collar particularly when working with a dog that has been abused and is spooked by restrictions around the back of the neck or around the throat. So a lead and collar, a toy and some food rewards are all you need.

There are other problems with gadgets: some are cruel, many don't work or are slight variations on a theme. A lot of gadgets on sale are purely money making projects hyped as the latest 'must have'. With so many to choose from, when a dog exhibits an unacceptable behaviour, by the time you've decided which of the multitude of gadgets or training aids to use you've lost the moment or spent a fortune on things that don't work at all, or only as a quick fix, working for a split second and then you're back to square one.

It's not what you say, it's what you do and it's not only what you do, it's what you feel. It all starts within you.

We hope that this book will reach anyone with an interest in dogs, either present or potential owners and give them an understanding of why dogs react the way they do to different situations and how to approach many behavioural problems. This will result in happy dogs and happy owners. Why do we humans get so stressed when things go wrong? Very often it's not the problem itself but the frustration in not knowing how to fix that small leak or put up a shelf that looks vaguely level. We can't help you with your plumbing or carpentry skills but we can help you with your dog.

This 'listening' theory is nothing new, it is the language of the canine. However in this book our aim was to write in such a way that you not only find it informative but also be able to put it into practice. We hope we have succeeded. It carries a serious message but will also hopefully make you smile in places too.

We will help you gain a better understanding of your dog and be able to enhance your relationship. We cover some frequently asked questions: some humorous, some embarrassing and some perplexing in the hope that you come to a better understanding of why your dog does what he does, and in many cases how to correct it.

Clients often contact us in despair: many of their problems involve aggression, dog on dog, dog on human, dog on absolutely everything and of course, inter-pack aggression. When dealing with aggression issues, although we will deal in depth with this subject we cannot cure these problems within the pages of a book. If you misunderstand our advice you could put yourself and others at risk. That is why on all television 'dog training' programmes there will be regular reminders on the screen like 'Don't try this at home' or 'Only attempt this under professional guidance'. Having said that, the advice we give to correct your dog's problems does not require you to use great physical strength and our method does not put you at risk. We wouldn't tell anyone to do anything that we wouldn't do ourselves. When dealing with aggression we need to know the dog and have a feel for it and the owner before advice is given...it is paramount we all get it right and that you, the owner, know exactly what to do and when.

Try phoning your doctor, telling them you have a bad headache and demanding a diagnosis and suitable treatment by phone. You would probably be told that you are either suffering from a hangover, migraine, a brain tumour or any number of other complaints and if you want to find out which, then you'd better make an appointment. It would be awkward to prescribe an aspirin and then have the patient drop dead because the doctor hadn't collected all the information. The doctor needs to see the patient, we need to see the dog.

When first asked to write a book, the look of horror on our faces must have been a picture! We can't do that, we're only humble PURE Dog Listeners! Well, it has been great fun and we have loved every minute.

Although we both have long histories in working with dogs and could impress you with lots of obscure technical terms we want this to be a user-friendly book. This certainly does not mean that we will 'dumb down' our writing, but be assured that when a technical term is used it will be fully explained. This is not a resolution to the United Nations but a book to help and guide at all levels. The truth of it all though is there are no major technical terms. We outline goals that are achieveable once you understand why your dog does what he does. You will then be in a better position to understand and help him to modify his behaviour, to fit in to our world and not panic. In so doing, both you and your dog will be happier. In your relationship, where there was once stress there will be harmony.

We hope this inspires you, helps you to learn and maybe even laugh a little. There are many training methods out there but canine communication is the method we abide by and believe wholeheartedly that unless your dog is suffering from a medical condition, you can overcome all behavioural issues. Simply put, we use this method because it works. If there is a sudden change in your dog's behaviour for no apparent reason, particularly unexplained or unprovoked displays of aggression then a trip to the vets for a checkup might be a wise move. Once the vet has given the all clear then we can make progress.

You have to want to make it happen and give it 100%, even though it's hard at times. Nothing worth having is easy. If you give up the dog has won and believe it or not he doesn't want that. You will be the underdog and you certainly don't want that either. The result is that you will both be unhappy.

We don't shout at fish or get upset when they don't do as we ask, or rabbits or hamsters or pigs or sheep...but the poor old horse and dog get the rough end of the deal as we expect them to do as we say, when we say, without any regard for their language. We try to bribe them with food or use strange gadgets to get them to respond. I don't bribe my children and I've never used a gadget to make them obedient: we built up a relationship based on trust and knowing their boundaries, which in turn makes them feel safe. So why not have a go and build the same trusting relationship with your dog. You will both smile and lead a happier stress-free life of understanding and companionship, which you both deserve.

So please read this with an open mind and let's make life a better place for our best mate: THE DOG.

This is our passion and our focus is on helping you mend your dogs.

PURE Dog Listening

How would you feel if you knew of a way
To persuade your 'bad' dog to do all that you say?

No more shouting and screaming and tearing of hair
But a way to proceed that is gentle and fair

"You've got to be joking" I'm hearing you say
"I've asked all the experts - there's only one way"

A bad dog must learn, and he'll understand force
Then he'll show you respect, as a matter of course

And what if I told you that this isn't true
All you'll teach him is fear, never friendship with you?

If you trouble to learn how to see through his eyes
He can do nothing right no matter how hard he tries

He can't understand how you want him to act
You are human, he's dog, and you can't beat that fact

He is not your sworn foe, so why treat him like that?
Do you want a true friend, or a beaten doormat?

So here's an idea, and please give it a thought
Why not simply discard all the things you've been
taught?

There's a much better way, and I promise you this
If you listen to us, there's a pathway to bliss!

Keep a true open mind, it really will serve you well
And learn the kind way that we call PDL!

By Leslie Harris

HAs your dog trained you ??

Look in to my eyes.

CHAPTER 1

From a dog's perspective

We have great difficulty with some clients persuading them that their dog is not a little furry human, often saying, "He's my baby. He understands everything I say," or "He knows he's been naughty for stealing that biscuit." But he's not a baby, he's a dog, a canine, a completely different species, one with its own language that is very subtle and has its own code of conduct. Dogs adhere to their code far more than we humans adhere to ours. We'll be polite most of the time but if we can't be bothered or are feeling a bit frazzled, so what? A dog will always do the right thing but it will be the right thing according to canine etiquette.

When a client has a problem with their dog's behaviour they ask why the dog has acted that way. "Why does he do that?" they say. The answer is always the same: Because he's a dog, not a furry human and that particular canine behaviour is what dogs do. We do tend to anthropomorphise our pets because we think that it helps our understanding of this different species we've taken into our home. Sadly it often leads to confusion - we've had dogs as companions for thousands of years, they are man's best friend, so obviously we think exactly the same. What makes us happy will make our dogs happy. What we regard as good manners so will our dogs. This is where it all starts going wrong. Picture the scene: rich, Great Aunt

Nelly comes for afternoon tea. The family dog is doing a bit of self grooming. He enthusiastically licks his rear end and then rushes over to Aunt Nelly to greet her and give her a big wet kiss. You get cut out of the will and get angry with the dog who responds with "What?" because he doesn't know what he's done wrong. It's normal to groom in this matter and you've always encouraged him to approach visitors to 'be friendly'. Well, it didn't work this time, did it?

As PURE Dog Listeners we are Consultants in Canine Communication so we use our skills to motivate a dog to tell you what life is like from a dog's perspective.

"Hello, my name is Spot and I'm a dog. Just that! a dog. I won't tell you what breed I am because then you'll expect me to behave in a particular 'breed specific' way only and I'm just a dog.

I was born at a very early age, one of a litter of seven. I had three brothers and three sisters and we were brought up by our mum: she was lovely, a good parent. We never knew our father - we've been told that he just turned up one night with a bottle of Blue Nun and a bunch of flowers from a garage forecourt. After some talk with mum about 'respecting her in the morning' he was off never to be seen again. Sixty-four days later we were born.

We stayed with mum for eight weeks and it was a very important time. She taught us as much as she could about how to behave and how to survive once we'd left home. Of course at that time we didn't know we would be leaving. We thought that we'd be staying together in a family/pack so that we could look after one another.

I didn't always get on with my brothers and sisters. Sometimes the games would get rough and one of us would get hurt. Mum explained that puppies had sharp teeth for that very purpose, teaching us that biting can cause pain. We learned not to bite our brothers and sisters too hard. If we did they would refuse to play with us and we didn't want that. Mum also explained that the rough and tumble was a grounding in hunting. She also told us that dogs had areas of loose skin so that puppies could hang on to it without causing damage.

While I was still with my mum there was this strange creature that would appear from time to time. It stood on its hind legs and mum said it was a 'Human'. Well this human seemed alright: it would supply food and clean up but left us pretty much alone until that fateful day.

One morning it got very noisy with lots humans looking at us and pointing. They come in different shapes and sizes. Mum explained that they are called 'men' and 'women' and their puppies are called 'children' and come in two models: boys and girls. I didn't like this at all: the humans made lots of loud strange noises and were leaning all over us. They picked me up and pushed their faces right up to mine. They kept making eye contact, which to a puppy is very scary. My brother Rex had some humans looking at him too. They were much more thoughtful, sitting near Rex but didn't put any pressure on him. They just waited for him to realise that they weren't a threat. I wish they'd told the humans with me the best way to behave. Suddenly it was all over, I was parted from my mum and brothers and sisters. I was taken by a man and a woman with a boy and a girl. I was really frightened. They took me to a new place full of strange sights sounds and of course smells. I was nervous and soon added my own smell to let them know I'd arrived. The humans got very angry. They shouted at me and rubbed my nose in the area where I'd marked.

They do a lot of this shouting and general noise making. It seems to be the way they communicate with one another. They've tried it on me but I just don't understand and then they get angry again. Sometimes they tap me on the nose or bottom or shake me and then they might pick me up and try to be my friend. I'm just so confused, the rules keep changing. They give me a biscuit from a plate on the table: that's nice, but when I help myself to another they shout at me. They keep calling my name but when I respond they don't do anything…"Spot, Spot, Spot, Spot." If I could I'd say to them, "Yes, I know what my name is. What do you want?" I've learned a few of their sounds have some meaning such as my name. I know what 'Sit' means because they say it very sharply and force my backside down. They seem to think the louder the sound is the more I'll understand. I know that when they go on holiday rather than buy a phrase book they still speak

English to the locals. They just speak it louder and slower. Do they think I'm a French shopkeeper?

I know that they're not bad people and that most of the time they are kind but they just seem to think that I should understand these funny noises they make. They lead very complicated lives but as I said earlier I'm just a dog, a simple animal and as long as I've got some food, know how to get some more, have time to play with the rest of the pack, have someone who'll know what to do if things get dangerous and be really sure where I and all my pack fit into the scheme of things, then I'm happy.

After a while following a visit to a strange place called 'the vet' my humans, I call them 'mine' because although they are completely disorganised, I've become very fond of them and feel responsible for them because I can't leave them to their own devices: they'd only get themselves into trouble...anyway, where was I? After the vet visit my humans took me out from our den for the first time and for some reason they tied me to them with a tether of some sort from my collar to their hand. I was a bit wary at first but soon started to enjoy it. I pulled to see what was around the next corner because I needed to know that I wasn't leading my pack into danger. Well that wasn't a good move because there was another of their loud noises and I got pulled back very hard: not very nice. I tried going ahead a few more times because that's my job, to be alert to danger, to protect the pack in anyway I can. Maybe I can do this by leading them to a safer place, keeping a low profile so we don't get involved in the potential danger or, as a very last resort, to get rid of the threat by verbal or physical aggression.

Now, I know what I'm doing, and why. As I told you I'm just a dog and live a very simple life. I'm really good at being a dog, it's probably my best point. I am however rubbish at being a human and that's the way my humans seem to think I should act, so when I pull forward again I get yanked back. When I stop pulling they make nice sounds and sometimes give me a bit of food. They mean well, but so do I and nature tells me I have to be out in front because none of these humans know how to make sure our pack survives. If they're not going to do the job then I've got to. The problem is that I don't understand the human world: there are loads of strange and scary sights and sounds when we leave the den. Big metal boxes on wheels that are noisy, fast and come very close. I jump up at them to see them off but get told off. I jump up at my humans to reassure them but again get told off. What am I supposed to do? I only want to please.

We then get to a big space and my human unties me. Wow, what a lovely feeling: I'm free and can run around and have fun. What's that over there? It's a squirrel. Game on! Off I go, I'll soon have lunch sorted and be very popular. My humans are making a lot of noise but instead of standing back there making a lot of fuss they should be over here backing me up. Now I know it's not a herd of buffalo but it's still hard to surround a squirrel on my own, particularly if he's up a tree throwing nuts at me.

Because of the lack of support from my pack the squirrel escaped but never mind, on my way back to my pack - still being very noisy - I find a nice really ripe dead rabbit. That'll do, if we can't have squirrel stew perhaps they'll like rabbit ragout. As I approach the pack with my prize they look both angry and horrified. When I push the rabbit into their groins they are quite ungracious in their response to this gift.

They took me to a place called 'Obedience Class', which I found rather confusing. Although I now realise there are some really good ones, the class I attended seemed a bit pointless to me. It appears that to humans it is vital that their dog goes to the village hall every Thursday evening and walks around in a circle for an hour in the company of some other dogs before going home again. Strange creatures these humans, aren't they? I don't know any of these dogs, they're not from my pack. Some are alright but others are troublemakers or just confused. Sometimes there are fights and the human in charge gets angry and tells one of the humans to leave and not bring their dog again. It seems that the trouble or lack of progress is never the fault of the head human who they call 'Instructor', but that of the dog's human. The Instructor never says, "We'll try something different to get over this problem." They always say, "Well, if you will get a (fill in choice of breed here) what do you expect? You'll never train a..." That's why I never tell anyone my breed - I don't want any trouble. My mum said to me, "Never discuss politics, religion or breeds with anyone."

As the days went by, I started to understand more of the sounds that humans make and tried my hardest to do things they ask. I walk close on walks, I sit when they ask, and go to my bed. I still chase things out and about, it's fun and I feel free, even if I do get a stern telling off when I get back…surely one day they will be pleased with what I have brought back to eat.

I felt they needed me to do more, so I let them know when there is danger about. If something is outside and I can hear it, I shout to let them know and they shout too…I've alerted them to danger and they are now joining in…great…OH!! Not so great…they are now shouting at me, panicking, so I'll shout louder, "do they want me to shout more?" Oh I don't know, but what I do know is that I'm frightened and they are frightened and I need to protect us all!

I can't relax during the day, not knowing what is going to happen or what they are going to do. I can't eat my food in the morning as I'm rather on edge. "What will today bring?" I follow them wherever they go in the house, just to make sure they are okay…no idea what I would do if anything went wrong, but at least they will know that I'm looking out for them.

I sit close and lean on them when we are in the den: they seem to like the reassurance that I'm there to protect them. See, I do fit in, but it's a hard job. I've always got to be alert and don't really relax until the evening when we are all in and they relax in front of this weird wobbly box that booms out strange sounds...I hate it and shout now and again when it is on. Not sure what it is, but it knows if it puts a step wrong I'm the one it has to deal with. Not that I'll have a clue what to do...but I have warned it. I hit it once and my humans hit me and shouted at me: I won't do that again...still hate it though and have to be on my toes just in case.

When they sleep, I can then sleep. But like any good parent I'll be there for them. That's what they want I'm sure.

We go for nice walks now on the lead: I've learnt to stay by their sides. But if there is something out there that I think could be a threat then I'll pull on that lead like you wouldn't believe. I've got to: it's my job to protect. They have given me no good reason to think otherwise. I don't understand them in the slightest. However I have food and a bed and we play games and do lots of stuff I enjoy. Always on the look out though, for things that may threaten our family.

One day when I was out for my walk who should I bump into but my brother Rex. We had a great time racing around and catching up on old times. You remember I told you how different the people who took Rex were to the pack that I joined? Well, Rex has really landed on his paws. I love my humans to bits but they drive me crazy with their inconsistency. They try hard but just as we seem to be getting somewhere they get it wrong again. They are kind, caring, but oh so confused.

Rex tells me that from day one his humans never told him to do something he didn't understand, instead they showed him. They didn't keep talking at him in a language he didn't understand but communicated with a lot of non verbal signals. 'Body language' I think you humans call it. As a result when Rex is spoken to by his human it's always good stuff. "Fetch." "Come." "Good boy." And so when Rex hears his name called his response is "What can I do for you?" Whereas when my name is called I think…

It seems that Rex's owner talked to something called a 'PURE Dog Listener' and got lots of advice and information from them which made life so much easier for both Rex and his man. The good news is that we often meet at the park now and while Rex and I play, our humans talk. Rex's human has started telling mine about the techniques he used and things are looking promising. Each time I come back from playtime with Rex my human is just that little bit more switched on. We may be getting somewhere. Watch this space."

The Trouble With Humans

Fern and I have been digging
We're having a great deal of fun
Fern thinks that her hole is the biggest
But I'm pretty impressed with my one

Our noses are beautifully muddy
Our paws are a nice shade of black
"Hey mum, come and look what we're doing"
NOW, WHY DID SHE GIVE US A SMACK?!!

And that is the trouble with humans
Sometimes they are no fun at all
She's so busy messing our holes up
She won't even play with the ball!

Well, I'm thinking "What would make her happy?"
When I tread on a very dead rat
Just the thing! Now who could stay angry
When they're given a present like that?!

Ohhh! It really smells lovely
My whole body itches to roll!
But no, I mustn't be selfish
A present is much better whole!

So gently I pick up my present
And proudly I march through the door
I remember my excellent manners
And gallantly offer a paw

WELL!! Not quite the reaction I wanted
Not what I expected at all!
A biscuit perhaps, or a thank you
Well, anything else but this roar.

"Oh Ria, what have you been doing
The whole house smells of death and decay!
AND WHAT IS THIS HORRIBLE OBJECT?
For goodness sake, take it away!"

And that is the trouble with humans
You give them your personal best...
Well, in future I don't think I'll bother
Where's my basket? I need a long rest.

By Leslie Harris

CHAPTER 2

How communicating on your dog's level
can help you in your life with your dog

All problems with your dog boil down to a communication issue. You are talking a language they don't understand, and they are talking a language you don't understand.

It has to be the responsibility of the more adaptable party - with the capacity to be pro-active not reactive and also with the capacity to think logically - to learn the language of the dog. Then, there will be harmony, and each will be able to understand what is expected of the other, and who is there to look after whom. It is not just down to who feeds and walks your dog - if only it were that easy - it runs far deeper than that! It's how you respond in a way the dog can understand. You have to show them you respect their ways and their instincts and work with those instincts, not against them: to bring harmony to the relationship. The word relationship is the key, just as in your relationships with other humans whether friends or loved ones, it's a two way street. You need to make your contribution to the relationship everyday. We've all seen what happens when one side of a partnership decides they don't have to make an effort. It never really matters what your dog does, it matters more how you respond to those actions.

To a dog everything is about survival, not only theirs

but the whole pack as well. Everything is subordinated to the survival of the pack. Nothing else matters: if a pack member has to die to ensure that the pack goes on then that is a price worth paying. All canines approach this with the same attitude whether one of the Queen's Corgis, a Hollywood starlet's 'handbag dog', a rough sleeper's crossbreed dog or your family pet. Dogs are programmed by thousands of years of nature to survive. We humans by and large have lost those skills. Most dogs if abandoned in the New Forest would survive - they would quickly realise that their human isn't going to be along anytime soon with their food. The dog would seamlessly slip into survival mode and he would hunt and scavenge to live. He might even join up with other dogs to form a mutually supportive pack and from there would develop a hierarchy. Consider a similar scenario involving a human. For an experiment we could take anybody from their centrally heated home in just the clothes they were wearing at the time and transport them to a car park in the forest in November. Before leaving we could search them and remove all money, watches, mobile phones and debit and credit cards and tell them they had to survive without any outside help. We could tell them that we'd collect them in March, but we'd probably have a long fruitless wait. We humans, for the most part, have lost those vital skills.

The world we live in is completely alien to the dog - they do not understand about locks on our doors and that others in close proximity are generally not a threat. We live close to our neighbours in our community which can be unsettling for some dogs. The pack has to be protected, the den, the territory i.e. its larder. Our territories are much smaller than they would instinctively be comfortable with - *we* have a food store and can buy and barter for food (the source of survival) but there is no bartering or buying or selling in the wild. We have to remember that we have come a long way from our origins and dogs have not. Their basic instincts are still all they live by.

We have adapted over time to living closer together and building communities where we rely on many more individuals, companies and strangers than in ages past. We are still territorial and protect our own so we may feed, clothe and house our family in a secure and safe environment. Try walking through a strange inner city area late at night. Maybe you've missed the last train home. Who do you approach for directions? Even more worrying, who do you avoid? Which road leads to safety and which to bandit country? Dogs in our world are put in this position daily.

It is too much to expect other species to understand the world we now live in: it is for us to adapt our communication skills to show them that we are in control and they are safe in our hands - that the protection of the pack/family is our responsibility. We are the decision makers and can take the pressure off them in this way. We have to show the dog that we also will be there to lead them and they just have to follow - if we give them this assurance then they will relax by our side in the knowledge that they are protected and safe. We deal with those situations which they do not yet understand or when they do not have the skills or life experience to be able to make informed decisions.

PURE Dog Listening tecnhniques provide a method for life which needs to be adopted as an ongoing process by the whole family. In the wild the leader in the pack never has a day off: if they did they would lose their role. The process will soon become second nature and enables further advanced training to take place in a stress-free environment. As with learning any new skill you will at times make mistakes...remember when you learnt to drive? If you do get something wrong, don't beat yourself up and think that it's the end of the world, but learn from the experience. If you notice another family member 'getting it wrong' point it out to them but do not treat this as a point scoring exercise. In the same vein, should you slip up and have it pointed out, do not get defensive, take note and move forward. The aim is to have a happy and well balanced dog, so let's leave our egos behind while practising.

You will, we hope, follow this method and have a truly wonderful relationship with your dog because for the first time you will really understand him. Your dog will be happy because the stress will be taken from his shoulders and he can pass the baton of responsibility to you. There are other benefits, you will not only understand your dog but others as well. You'll see Mr Macho in the park posturing and shouting at his dog and you'll smile to yourself and think 'If you knew what your dog was really saying to you, then you wouldn't look so pleased with yourself'...

So we all know dogs don't talk. Maybe they utter the odd bark, howl or make comfortable contented noises, but the bulk of their communication is body language. We too communicate a lot with both conscious and sub-conscious body language. If the words don't match the body language then we become unbelievable and untrustworthy and we pick up on these 'tells' instinctively. How many times have you watched an interview on television and just knew without a doubt that the interviewee was a liar or at best economical with the truth? It's instinct, one of the few survival tools we humans have partially retained.

Dogs can't talk, however they do have an ability to understand some of our spoken words. They are real experts in picking up and interpreting our body language whether for good or ill. If you unwittingly give your dog a wrong signal don't be surprised if he behaves in a way that you find unacceptable. You told him to do it or at the very least signalled that it was alright to do it. Let's show them how we wish them to behave, how to fit in. We cannot tell them by using words or bully them, we cannot expect respect if we do not show them respect or if we try to dominate...we have to kindly show them in a way they understand what is acceptable and what is not. Is it not said that we should lead by example? Be kind, considerate and patient with dogs and people alike, and you will reap the rewards. Be a bully or expect all cultures and species to learn our language and you have set yourself up for failure…and you have failed your dog.

It's often said of the English that we expect everybody else to learn our language. Wouldn't it be great to show respect for each and every one out there if we tried to learn at least just a little of their ways and spoken word. It would be a gesture of goodwill and demonstrate respect for others. If we did this we would be more likely to be accepted and be shown mutual respect. Go in shouting English at others with no regard for their limited understanding and you will get little or no respect at all. Indeed, you are more likely to encounter resistance than co-operation. This is just as true of dogs as it is of humans. Of course there are so many human languages that with the best will in the world we can only brush the surface. With dogs however there is only one language: Canine. Learn it in London and you can use it in Lisbon, Las Vegas or Lille. Wherever you are you'll be understood.

Learn your dog's body-language so you understand what your dog is thinking when undesirable behaviour hits. Also its important to be able to ascertain whether your dog is relaxed and happy. It's true that a lot of what we have learnt is from observing wolves and other canines in the wild and domestic situations, but we can also look to ourselves and see that we react in situations in a similar way when we are in over our heads too. The difference is that we can be pro-active if we think and reason, then come to a logial conclusion before we react.

Dogs understand their own body language. We have many different breeds out there and they are not there through natural selection: we have selectively bred to all different shapes and sizes. What we have not changed is the brain make-up. They all think the same: who's protector and who's provider, as we do too. Different breeds tend towards different behavioural issues, but it is all for the same reasons: dogs will consider 'Who can I count on?', 'Am I in charge?' or 'Can it eat me or can I eat it?'...

Just doing 'obedience' basics such as 'sit', 'stay' and 'heel' is like getting your best friend to do the same for no good reason. The only reason you gave them is 'Because I told you to!' or 'Because I bribed you', or your approach might be steeped in 'Do what I want or I'll hurt you or shout at you...a lot!'

As far as PURE Dog Listeners are concerned, we have to start way further back than that. Gain trust and respect and build up a trusting relationship. The 'sit', 'stay', recall, 'heel' etc. are the skills we humans think are needed to pass canine control exams but you don't have to be a control freak. Don't try to micromanage every action of your dog's life. Don't nag. It's nice to have a dog that will follow these simple requests, but get this through co-operation. In order to teach these exercises in any environment your dog needs to choose their teacher as the one they ultimately trust and feel safe with. They should be the ones that a dog can relax and learn with, who explains in a way that they understand what is expected of them.

There is a school with a prospectus that reads: 'If the pupil does not learn the way we teach, then we will teach the way the pupil will learn'. Never a truer word spoken or written…help them want to learn, inspire them and they will learn, not by bullying or intimidation but by nurturing the natural abilities and instincts of their learning skills. Work with them and at their speed, don't push them beyond their learning pace and they'll get there in the end. Be patient. Work with, not against them. Be kind, considerate, inspiring and encouraging. Don't bribe but do reward.

We understand what a dog is thinking by its reactions. A dog is a dog at the end of the day, as we are all humans. It is true that certain breeds tend to display different behaviours, this is because we humans have tinkered with nature and produced retrievers, herders, guarders, hunters, terriers. The list is endless. They are all dogs but may also have a bolt-on retrieving or herding instinct put there by man. When it really matters the bolt-on drops away and the dog reverts to pure canine survival. To do our job we look beyond the breed to the individual personalities of each dog. There are shy guard dogs, aggressive lap dogs and everything in between.

Different people react to situations depending on personality and up-bringing. Why should any other species be any different?

Why do we feel we have to train dogs, why can't we

just guide them in a way that they understand to fit in to our world? We let other domestic animals be themselves to a far greater degree. Chickens are allowed to dig up the garden because that's what chickens do. It is accepted that cats do their own thing too, so why are we so obsessed with controlling dogs?

PURE Dog Listeners let a dog be just that, a dog. We bring it up gently with boundaries, consistency and love. There are no tricks. It is straight forward if you open your mind to learning. This is the way we used to be with dogs before we brought them into our homes and they had no specific job but to just be there for us. So that's what we have done, we have humanised them and they are there for us and our emotional needs...which is where it goes so wrong for them.

We are not saying you can't love your dog, cuddle your dog, kiss it or have it on your bed. The ground rules in your house are the ones that you set. It's your house, your dog, your rules. The only rule that you must always adhere to in order to ensure a harmonious relationship is that your dog works around you. Not you around your dog. You can have as much interaction as you want, probably more than you do now because it will be on your terms. All we say is make sure it is you who calls a dog into your space, don't let the dog call the shots. This will show you to be a credible leader and reassure your dog that you are there for it, not the other way around. This creates a happy dog without the pressure of having to look after you.

Yes, there are assistance dogs, helping people to lead independent lives - they do help us but they are given 'games' to play that are rewarded. These 'games' might involve teaching how to switch on a light, helping someone get dressed, guiding someone…they have to be fun and trained in such a way so the dogs do not put a foot wrong. So they have time on duty and time off duty when they can just be themselves. They have a work/life balance.

Police dogs need, of necessity, to be under control but all their training, whether tracking, agility, searching, man-work (chasing and biting) or any of the more specialist tasks is presented and completed as a game. A fun approach to learning, in a manner that uses a dog's natural instincts to the handler's ends, is the strategy applied for the benefit of the public.

Pet dogs need stimulation too - team building games and fun walks - and time to rest and sleep in peace and quiet. To be able to enjoy a game a dog needs to be relaxed, but some dogs won't play or can't play. Apart from the older infirm dogs or ill dogs for that matter, the main reason a dog won't play is that either they are very stressed or it is too preoccupied with looking after you and the rest of the family.

CHAPTER 3

Canine Communication with PURE Dog Listeners

What Canine Communication with PURE Dog Listeners certainly **IS**:

o Kind, pro-active and teaches dogs to self-control
o Non aggressive and only uses appropriate correction
o Intimidation, drug and gadget free
o Dog friendly, because it uses a dog's natural instincts and language
o Holistic
o A way to create a calm and happy dog and owner
o A method that needs a sense of calm, consistency, empathy, patience and a positive mental attitude
o Based on understanding dogs and their natural behaviour
o A method that really works if you are dedicated
o Value for money

It **DOES NOT**:

o Enforce your will on the dog
o Turn dogs into robots
o Offer a quick fix without effort on the part of the owner (There is no fixed timeframe.)

and **IS NOT:**

- o A way of dominating your dog
- o Based on ignoring dogs
- o Cruel in any shape or form

Also there is **NO NEED TO:**

- o Tease with food
- o Click your fingers
- o Poke your dog in the ribs
- o Force your dogs to 'confront their fear'
- o Use any verbal correction in any shape or form
- o Exhaust your dog so he sleeps

We are very clear to everyone we come in contact with what our philosophy is and that we use no cruel methods or harmful equipment at any time.

We use the term 'Dog Listener' because it's non confrontational and because most people, and that includes trainers of all kinds, spend a huge amount of time talking to and at their dog without taking time to interact with and watch the subtle messages via body-language that the dog is sending back. There is a conversation taking place here and most people miss it. In so doing they also miss much of the joy of dog ownership and the chance to deal with any problems in the early stages.

We further refined our name to PURE Dog Listeners to stress that we were not, as some using the same 'job description' were, crossing into other methods and 'mixing and matching' which only leads to confusion.

We are not in opposition with other dog professionals whether they are trainers, behaviourists, whisperers, listeners, or go by any other title. There are as in every walk of life those who are good, bad or indifferent. We will however have nothing to do with those who use cruel methods. Our only aim is to help dogs and their owners. There are sadly a few characters in the dog world that are incredibly hostile to any method that is different to the one they use. If what they are doing works why would they be concerned about what others are doing?

Whatever title we choose we are all teachers. To gain knowledge all that is needed is a good teacher and a desire to learn. All our members are subject to continuing assessments to ensure that standards are maintained and improved. As for the students there is no problem because the dog part of the team is generally happy to learn and once the humans realise that they have a problem their minds are open as a result.

As the founder members of PURE Dog Listeners we have a long and proven track record of dealing with dogs of all sizes and shapes and all manner of problems. Although I've had dogs all of my life I have earned my living from dogs since 1977 and as a Police Officer also dealing with a range of people in different situations. Caroline also has a strong practical dog background going back many years. In addition to her Dog Listening work she has trained working dogs and given displays at country shows. She also worked as a nurse so, again, experience in both canine and people skills is present.

When a PURE Dog Listener deals with a client they go to their home and see the dog in its home environment with the whole family present. They will spend as much time as it takes to get to the route of the problem and ensure that the client has all the information they need to get the dog to change their behaviour of its own free will. Everything is done in front of the client so they can see that it works. There are no secrets: we use PURE Dog Listening because it is natural and it works. (It does not involve any aversive training.) Once the consultation is concluded the client gets a comprehensive 'Action Plan' that is individual and relevant to the particular client. The client then has free back up for the life of the dog.

We never leave a client until they are happy that they understand how they are going to move forward, and never tell a client that their time is up. I recently did a nine hour consultation but the client only paid the set fee. All PURE Dog Listeners put the dogs' interests first and if a job takes longer than anticipated then it does.

Does one size fit all? If so, how? You will be surprised maybe to hear that it will! This is not breed specific, it is dog specific. All dogs think like dogs!

The core of canine communication incorporates five main areas:

1) Who is in control at feeding time
2) Who makes decisions about danger
3) Who leads the walk
4) Who calls the shots on rejoining and affection
5) Who is team leader when it comes to play

This is our framework, our starting point and to that we must stay PURE. If, however, we only had to routinely do 'The Five', like a mechanic opening and fitting a box of brake pads in a garage, it would be easy.

It is the variations in the way the dogs test us and how, when we deal with one challenge they can instantly throw us another. The different personalities of the owners, their lifestyles as well as their dogs all pose the question to us: "You've dealt with all manner of problems before, but this one is really different. Let's see you solve this one." That is the real challenge and what makes being a PURE Dog Listener so fascinating.

We stick with 'The Five', but in the words of Clint Eastwood (to quote from Heartbreak Ridge, when the Marine Sergeant character he played was teaching his platoon that you can't always do things as per the book, without any leeway whatsoever) in response to "What do we do?" was always "Adapt, Improvise, Overcome." If we have to alter our approach it doesn't matter as long as we stay true to our philosophy.

Does Dog Listening work?

As with everything in life it is what you put in to it that counts. If you have a consultation with a PURE Dog Listener, then you have their advice for life. They will never come up with a "I don't know what to suggest next!" or disappear into the sunset having written you a report or charge you for advice by phone or e-mail following your consultation.

We don't do phone consultations. We have to meet you, observe your dog and get a good feeling for his personality, the problems, your home and life.

This method does not work with some dogs. It works with ALL dogs irrespective of breed, age or gender. Stick with it and it will work. If you give up when the going gets tough (and it probably will!) then you will fail.

Please note that, as mentioned already, if your dog has a medical problem giving rise to unacceptable behaviour then that is a job for your vet initially.

CHAPTER 4

Leadership

We will talk a lot about leadership throughout this book because it is a subject that is essential to all dogs' survival and sense of well being. There must never be any doubt as to who the team leader is. In canine terms the leader is called the Alpha but this can be the cause of much misunderstanding. When humans think of themselves as Alpha they can so often think this means doing a lot of shouting and maybe even manhandling. 'Sit! Stay! Come! Down! Go to your bed! Stand on one leg and whistle Dixie! Breathe in and out!' Do you know what? None of that impresses any dog. You can't make, no matter how much you shout, any dog see you as leader. You can however show them by your actions throughout each and every day that you are worthy of the position, that you will ensure the survival and continuance of the pack. So it doesn't matter to a dog what you're called, rather what you are. So we can use a variety of terms: Alpha, Leader, Boss, Head Honcho, Guv'nor or, our favourite, Team Leader. Pick the one you like that suits your personality. Hopefully you won't choose 'Master'.

If you're not the leader at the moment, how do you achieve that position? How do we gain advancement in the human world? It doesn't matter if we're talking about becoming the head of a multi-national company or simply moving from junior office boy to senior office boy. We get promoted because maybe we're the boss' son, we sleep with the boss, we play golf with him or maybe we're the only candidate with a particular qualification. We may be the most inefficient person in the company but we can wave our certificate in the air. We may just interview very well or simply have been in post longest so it's our turn. In some cases, however, it can actually be because we're the best person for the job.

In the canine world you get the job because you're the best person for it. You don't get the job because your dad had it before you but because the other members of the pack approach you, indicate when things get tough, and (it really matters) that you are the one they look to for a decision and to save the day. You are the brightest, strongest and the best hope for the future. The leader is chosen by the pack, not forced on it.

Imagine being shipwrecked…among the survivors from First Class is a self important, self promoting multi-millionaire and maybe a 'Super Model', both used to always having what they want instantly, anytime, day or night. Among the other survivors is maybe a gamekeeper, a carpenter, a woman who is a keen gardener who cooks her own produce (who knows what is edible and what is not), or maybe a doctor or nurse. Now who would be 'Team Leaders'? Would the survivors choose someone because they had lots of money in the bank thousands of miles away that was of no use in the present situation? Or maybe they'd choose someone whose contribution to society was being thin and wearing a frock while staring blankly into the distance. My best guess is that they would look around the group and choose those who could find or grow food, build shelter or keep the group healthy.

Those of you who are parents will remember those heady days early in your children's lives when they thought mum and dad were perfect and knew everything. Then of course they get older and realise you know nothing...but all is not lost. You can reclaim a bit of your bruised ego here, because if you consistently give your dog the right signals then the dog will always think you know everything. When a problem occurs, no matter how big or small, your dog will look to you and say, "Decision please?" You will of course know how to respond, both because you will now be the Team Leader but also because you have read this book.

Howdy!...

CHAPTER 5

Dog breed misconceptions

Dogs have been selectively bred for thousands of years, sometimes by inbreeding from the same ancestral lines, sometimes by mixing dogs from very different lines. The process continues today, resulting in a tremendous variety of dog breeds. Many of the pedigree dogs we see around us now are fairly recent arrivals, manufactured by the top of the food chain, man. One breed, probably one the most easily recognisable dogs on the planet, the German Shepherd, has only been around since 1899...the blink of an eye in real terms.

All dogs whatever breed, have the same brain make-up: we have just changed the way they look. This being so, all breeds speak the same language and understand each other. We being humans talk human but whatever spoken language we use, the dog does not understand it. A lot of our communication is non verbal: about 75%. A dog's communication is nearly completely non-verbal. With this in mind, it becomes obvious that the way to get through to your dog must be to apply a non-verbal approach. So, show them how to behave. The spoken word is meaningless to a dog. They learn words by repetition, but only by the sound, not the spelling! 'Sit', 'stay', 'down' and 'heel' are useful things to have your dog understand but where we so often go wrong is to start by imposing our will on them. It is important that a dog be able to fit into our world and so be acceptable wherever we go. If we start by showing the dog that we are able to make all the big decisions then, rather than using compulsive methods to get compliance, we achieve this within our everyday work with dogs. The dog is happy to 'come', 'sit' and 'stay' because you have shown that you will be responsible for every aspect of the welfare of the pack. Who wouldn't want to be with the person that keeps them safe? Obedience training is good but it is the foundation upon which these exercises are taught that is the most important.

As previously mentioned certain breeds may tend towards certain behaviours. But within breeds there are many personalities, as there are within litters. It is the personality that counts, as it does with humans. This is what we concentrate on. It is not a breed issue, it is a personality thing. It is often the case that a dog behaves in a certain way not because they are a specific breed, but because a human has decided that he requires a certain behaviour from a dog, so he buys a specific breed hoping he'll get it. This is not likely to be a problem if you want to go for nice walks in the country, perhaps drop into a pub on the way home and so choose a Labrador. If you are not active and live in town and decide a lap dog is right for you, perhaps consider getting a smaller dog as a companion - no problem there. Either way both dog and human need to understand one another for a fulfilling relationship.

Common Canine Misconceptions

A dog wagging its tail is a happy dog.

Of course dogs do wag when happy but also when they are biting. All a wag shows is that the dog is in a heightened state of awareness. It is what the other parts of the body are doing as well that tells the whole story. Stretch your eyes and see the bigger picture.

Grrr...!

Jack Russells and other Terriers can't be trained: they're snappy, it's in their nature.

Every generalisation has some basis in fact, so it is true to say that when a Terrier closes its jaws, it is done in a snappy way. This is purely because we have bred these dogs to catch rats and similar, so of necessity they have to be quick. How a dog reacts when dealing with a rat is entirely different to how they deal with a human. If you don't give a dog reason to bite, it won't. If you put it in a position where they have no option, then they will whatever the breed.

My dog is pleased to see me and he loves people, that's why he jumps up.

Now, I love meeting people, my children love seeing their friends and me hopefully too! But whenever we meet we do not jump and leap over each other, especially strangers. Neither do dogs to other dogs unless they have an issue. A gentle greeting, a little bottom sniffing is all that is required - we're talking about dogs here by the way! We humans will either hug, kiss, nod or shake hands depending how familiar we are with each other. It is all respectful of the individual's space and culture.

A dog leaping up at you is saying, "Me, me, me, me first!! Don't forget about me, I'm the most important." Greeting strangers like this is a dog questioning a stranger in its own and its owners personal space, and/or "talk to me first, I'm the important one." Reminiscent of an ill-mannered child trying to butt into a conversation all the time.

German Shepherd Dogs and other guarding breeds will always be aggressive.

Just think of how many of these dogs are used as Guide Dogs for the blind and other assistance dogs and how Police Dogs are used to find missing children. It would not be good for police public relations if the dog, having found the child, then ate it!! Parents tend to get a bit irritated by things like that!

A calm dog is depressed.

A calm dog is just that. Calm, contented and happy: in the knowledge that the stress of decision making has been lifted from his shoulders. We often see dogs tearing around in the park, jumping up or chasing a ball, ploughing into people and disturbing everyone else's playtime with their children or walk with their dog. Is this a happy dog? Possibly, possibly not...what he is, is living on adrenaline and lacking in self-control. Then there is the quiet plodder, sniffing here and sniffing there, fetching a ball and taking note of the world in a very laid back fashion, now he is most probably happy. You don't have to be firing off all cylinders to be happy, unless you're an adrenaline junkie that is.

You can't teach an old dog new tricks.

Dogs can learn at any stage of their life just as humans can. If I was told I couldn't go on a course because I was too old, I'd be a little put out and with current ageism legislation it might even be illegal to suggest such a thing! Okay, the older you are the longer it takes to break old habits and learn new things, but you'll get there in the end. It's the same for a dog: if he's been doing a certain behaviour for years it's going to take longer to correct it compared to a dog that has been doing the same thing for a very short time.

You have to train your dog to perfection by 18 months or you never will.

A dog is constantly learning. That's why they're such fun. Dogs mature at about 18 to 24 months of age. We visit every age with many varied problems and it's clear that there is no time limit to success - it depends on how well and quickly the owners adapt to the new PURE format and of course the personality of the dog in question. We get called out to see people with new puppies who want to tap into their dog's mind and ways, so they can bring up a puppy through to adulthood in a gentle way, resulting in a dog that has no issues.

An aggressive dog is a bad dog.

An aggressive dog is one that has been given the wrong information or placed in a situation where he feels that he has no option but to display aggression to survive or to protect other members of his pack. Put yourself in a position where you feel threatened, really threatened…what would you do? If you were with a trusted friend, maybe you'd make a different decision or leave the decision up to them. If you were a child with an adult you'd expect the adult to make the decision and keep you safe. Do you lead, follow or get out the way? A child would expect the adult to lead…do the same for your dog.

I have a Beagle so I will never stop it running off.

If you are a strong credible leader then your dog, whatever the breed, will want to be with you and will return when you call. The issue with such a dog is often far more than what some might call a 'breed characteristic'. I have had clients that have Dalmatians but these dogs don't feel the need to follow carriages all day! There are people who have gundog breeds and say that these dogs need to go on a shoot regularly and pick up game because that's what their dogs' parents did. Now how do the dogs know that? How many humans follow exactly the same occupation as their parents? As long as the human is not a drain on the rest of society then what they choose to do is of no concern to others. What the dog does need is stimulation in the form of games – 'seeking' games, 'retrieving' games (and it really doesn't matter what it picks up, a dead pheasant or an old purse is fine)...it's team work and getting the old grey matter working that really counts. For example, a German Shepherd doesn't need to go tracking for criminals just because that's what it's mum did, it needs to be engaged in proactive games that gets it thinking.

Some dogs are extremely fussy eaters.

Dogs can often be labelled as picky eaters. Why? Because they are anxious or signalling to you that they are taking control of feeding time. Many times we have been to consultations and been faced with a dog that does not eat well or grazes and in less than a week they are eating well with no issues.

All dogs love to be stroked by strangers.

Personal space is of huge importance to a dog because this is a key factor involved in its survival. If you enter any dog's personal space you are telling them that you have a lower status than them. You are of no account. If after giving that signal to a dog you then push your hand forward and touch him uninvited, depending on the personality of the dog, he may then back away, go into freeze mode or bite you. Try approaching a human in the street without invitation, telling them they're good looking and then stroking them. The odds are that you'd end up in hospital or at the police station! If a human wouldn't like it, why should a dog?

You wouldn't approach a wild animal in this way because you may well get bitten. Just because we have domesticated the dog, it doesn't mean it has forgotten how to survive. To put it another way, we all love a good massage but we're certainly not going to get a complete stranger to do it!!

I've got a Bichon Frise, a Chihuahua or a Yorkie,
so it is going to yap at everything.

Small dogs yap because they are small and therefore have a small voice box. It then follows that their bark will be sharp and piercing. If they were a Great Dane the bark would be a satisfying WOOF! The problem is not the key in which the bark is delivered - we can't change nature - but if you follow PURE Dog Listening techniques then the problem of constant barking by any breed will be resolved. It is generally a dog warning the pack that there is danger and telling the intruder to come no further. We must respond in the appropriate manner, as described in the section about 'Danger' in chapter 6.

Separation anxiety is the result
of my dog missing its leaders.

If a dog is confident in your abilities to both look after him and yourself, then he will be relaxed with or without you. If, however, your dog feels responsible for you (as you would a toddler) then it's in its nurturing nature to follow and be there for you. So if it can't follow you, it can therefore not look out for you, and will be anxious to know your whereabouts and what you are getting up to. Imagine if your toddler had locked himself in the kitchen, with the gas hob on. How would you react? To help your dogs be happy and relaxed whether with you or without you, then follow the advice in the five areas we have covered. Also pay attention to the section entitled 'Take the sting out of leaving' in chapter 7.

Dogs pull on the lead because they love their walks.

Walks should be a pleasure for both you and your dog. An opportunity to play 'follow my leader' and to enjoy each other's company. Pulling on a lead hurts. A big dog hurts YOU more than a little dog pulling, but in both cases it hurts the dog just as much. Stuck on a lead the dog can't get away if trouble strikes. If a dog was happy with their team leader's decision making skills, then it would not matter whether he was on or off lead as the dog would remain relaxed.

Dogs out there 'pulling' are dogs taking owners for a walk and for the most part do enjoy their walks, but are dragging you along to the place that they can be let off to free-run and play. Wouldn't it be great for you to enjoy your walk right from the beginning?

Dogs pulling towards other dogs, people, buses, maybe even barking too, are dogs on a mission, a mission to protect and check out the opposition. Being that packs do not naturally meet in the wild, it is natural for them to want to know 'who goes there?' You will find, even if as a puppy they were fine in the little puppy socialisation class you went to, as the puppy grows up it will be testing out your abilities as leader, testing boundaries. If he comes up with the answer that you are not an effective leader, then he has to assert himself. How he asserts himself - whether he follows through with the fight option, rather than just the checkout option - has a great deal to do with individual personality.

As far as lunging for buses, cars and bikes maybe even chasing them if they get the chance, we have to understand that these are all seen as a danger prompting a 'chase them out of town' attitude. Dogs do not understand our world, they never will, but as long as they feel safe by our sides then they will accept your decision and will feed off your calm demeanour.

Dog breed misconceptions

*Put a dog in a cage and it will cure
separation anxiety.*

Very rarely will this cure separation anxiety. What it
does do is save your kitchen from being damaged!

*It's a big mistake having two puppies from the same
litter, they join up in a pack against you.*

My next-door neighbour has twins and I didn't hear
anyone tell her to get rid of one and re-home it! With
puppies, choose the right personalities and you'll do
just fine. Yes, it is double the amount of hard work,
but if you have the time and even more patience,
then why not?

You'll never cure in-house fighting, just re-home one.

It's all down to management. It occurs because the
dogs are trying to assert themselves as leaders.
Most often we are called to homes when they have
had a new puppy and come 18 months to 2 years
this new kid on the block has matured and decides
it is going to be the decision maker. This manifests
itself in many ways, most often when the owners
enter, leave or are in the room. Most often the dogs
are fine when the owners are out of the equation. If
you manage the situation and show them that you
are the one to be looked up to and what they are
doing is neither necessary nor acceptable then this
behaviour will cease. They are trying out for the 'top
job' of protector and if you've got that job, then there
will be no discussion on the matter between them.

We can describe 'how' here, although it far better that you have a one to one practical consultation with a PURE Dog Listener to get it absolutely right.

In short, you have to work on the five areas with each dog, and separately when it comes to the walk, training and play. Play may set off fights as it is all about 'trophy winning' not merely a game when it comes to dogs with dogs. Try any 'walk training' separately as they will respond better singly without trying to out-do the other. We advise this even if your dogs do not have an aggression issue with each other, as one will progress quicker than the other and you do not have the complication of trying for 'front' position, however gently they may do it. It gives you time to evaluate each dog as an individual.

Pin-point the times that aggression arises: is it over food, toys or just when you are in a room, or when visitors arrive or just because one walked past the other?

Initially you must get the dogs to relax in each other's company - this may mean doing some silent zig-zag walking and use the 'Calm Hold' at either ends of the room or garden by taking the dog by the collar and drawing them to you and holding them firmly but not roughly at your side. Neither speech nor any eye contact are required. Have the aggressor on a trailing line at all times so if you see a stare or hear a grumble you can remove the dog from the room, without a word, into the downstairs loo if you have one, or another suitable room where he finds himself alone and pack-lost: children should not be allowed to carry this procedure out.

As time goes by and you are establishing a great relationship of trust and status in all areas, then the dogs will calm down and the fighting will stop as they accept your leadership.

There are cases though where the dogs just don't like each other and every now and again trouble rumbles on: this is when it can sometimes be kinder to re-home one of them.

I did a consultation with just such a duo: they were rescue dogs, one aged five years and the other seven years. The oldest just skulked about the place, avoiding eye contact or any contact at all actually. They had to be homed together as they'd always been together, when in actual fact it was very apparent that the older one had been walking on eggshells all of his life. The situation greatly improved by using PURE Dog Listening, however the older dog still didn't look terribly happy and the decision was made to re-home him to one of their friends who lived a quiet and uncomplicated life with no other dogs or children. He's a changed dog now and as happy as Larry.

Is a dog aggressive? Test it, take its food away!!

This is a complete 'No-No!' If you want to make a dog food aggressive then this is the way to do it!

I'm so confused....
Where's a PDL when you need one?!

CHAPTER 6

The Five Key Components of PURE Dog Listening

It is important to realise that this method is a way of life with your dog and it becomes easier and second nature to you as you make progress. Like learning any language it takes time and commitment to make progress. The first two to three weeks are always the hardest: there will be changes in your dog's behaviour, some good, some just different and some not as acceptable. All changes in our minds are 'good changes' as it means that you are getting through to your dog and it's having to think about its position within the family - remain that true leader and show him that this behaviour is not acceptable, and that behaviour is spot on. Then you are on the road to educating your dog to fit in with you and your world.

It is imperative that you cover all of the elements of the system. The temptation is to say, "My dog pulls on the lead, that's all I need to worry about." You will fail if you think like that. Every canine lives by the following rules, all of them, all of the time. This ensures survival. To only do part of the method and expect to succeed is like going to a driving school and telling them that you don't need to learn about braking, because you will be a careful driver... expecting to pass your test while lacking an essential piece of survival knowledge. What would your chances be?

If your dog is not getting the attention for doing something that it has before then it will try something else. If you cave in then the dog thinks…oh, you tried to do the job but you failed…I was the most persistent and have proven to be the better team leader.

You will have to show your dog many times in some instances what is correct and what is not: they are not going to get it in five seconds. So be patient and work with your dog and don't expect too much too soon.

Don't think you have a problem with your dog…think of it more as a challenge and you will succeed.

This way of communicating is quite easy to learn and very soon you will be able to interpret what your dog is doing and so what it is saying. The difficult part is to change to the new ways from your old ways. Be patient with yourself and it will happen. Canines talk with their body language and so must you for them to truly understand, and that is not by simply putting your hand up for a 'sit' as you go through a door - dogs don't tell dogs to 'sit', they show them they have priority as we will explain later. If you've ever seen your dogs together and one always goes through the door first, it is not because they have made the other 'sit', it is because they have earned respect. It is true that wolves and dogs do use aggression to get to the top and there is intimidation towards some pack members who push their luck, but they are good at 'dog talk' and we are only beginners and don't know it all and certainly do not need to resort to physical confrontation or domination. We can get through to a dog without using aggression or intimidation and forge a better relationship. That actually rings true for humans as well as dogs.

Remember...

- It takes no longer to think than it does to panic
- You are the Team Leader/Decision Maker
- Stop, Think and Deal with the situation

---

1)   FOOD

Before we go into detail about how to feed your dog, remember it is important for you to take care in deciding what to feed your dog. The cheapest or the most expensive is not always the wisest choice. You may choose a natural diet with mineral and vitamin supplements, a wet food diet with biscuit mixer or a dry complete diet. Whichever you choose, feed your dog twice a day as an adult: in this way it will be able to digest and utilise all the goodness from the food. By giving one large meal a day you are asking a lot of your dog's digestive system and he may not be able to utilise it all successfully. It is true that in wolf packs it is common to experience either feast or famine. We do not condition our domestic dogs like that, and by feeding twice a day they have fuel they can call on and don't get the drop in blood sugars that may result in behaviour problems. We get irritable when hungry and shaky too, so spread the load and split the amount you give your dog in two and feed twice a day. This also gives you another opportunity to give this powerful message of priority over feeding.

Priority Feeding

When we talk about food, what are the similarities between us and our dogs? Quite simply, the dog's relationship to food is completely different to ours, apart from, if we don't eat we die. That's it, everything else is completely different. We have meals at regular times because our lives are run by the clock. The canine eats when they can because they can never be sure when they will eat again. We, not our dogs, are the 'fussy eaters' and yet we live in a world of choice. Most households have a kitchen with fridge/freezer and cupboards full of food. The human can probably rustle up anything from cheese on toast to a three course meal. Even with all that choice someone is likely to say that there's nothing they fancy. No matter - most places have access to a late opening or even 24 hour supermarket. If we don't feel like going out, once again - no problem. We can pick up the phone and arrange home delivery of a pizza or an Indian or Chinese meal. Once our meal is ready we can sit around the dining table with friends and family and maybe a bottle of wine or we can relax in front of the TV with a pizza.

The Alpha eats first, takes the best bits, and also dictates in which order and how much the other pack members eat. This is one of the strongest signals you can give to your dog, and also one of the easiest to do. Don't stick to rigid mealtimes for your dog: in the wild their mealtimes are dictated by when or indeed if they catch anything and if there's enough to go around. If you always feed at a set time then you hand the 'power of food' to your dog, a huge signal. If you have young children a rigid canine feeding timetable can cause you more problems because the last thing that you will need if you have children off school with measles or similar, is a dog demanding to be fed because it's one minute past twelve, just when you're trying to dispense foul tasting medicine to resistant and sick children. The change doesn't have to be great, sometimes just a change of routine will do. If you feed your dog first thing in the morning before your shower then you could perhaps from time to time go to the kitchen, get yourself a drink, have a slice of toast, then feed him. Dogs are very good on picking up our routines, so if you always stir your tea three times, then have a slice of toast before feeding your dog, then as you wipe the last crumb from your lips, he will be there demanding.

When the humans in a pack eat, it is nothing to do with the dog. But when we feed our dogs it is vital that they understand that food comes courtesy of the leader i.e. that the leader has control over the food. The senior pack members always eat first, but what if you want to feed your dog at six and yourself at eight? No problem, remember your dog works around you not the other way around. When we talk about eating first we mean: a grape, a slice of apple, a small biscuit or maybe a square of chocolate, but not dog food! Any family member in the house at feeding time should take part in the feeding as this will reinforce their status. Before you go anywhere near the dog food, decide what you and other family members are going to have as your treat. If children are involved make sure that you choose something they like, we don't want the ritual disrupted because a child has been given something they hate. Put all the nibbles on a plate and place it on the surface where you will prepare your dog's meal. With any other family members, go to the kitchen or other feeding area. Do not speak to or make eye contact with the dog. You can talk amongst yourselves. Do not make your dog 'sit' and 'wait', 'give a paw' or perform any other party trick as this is a human perception of control.

Prepare your dog's food in full view. When it's ready you have 'priority of feeding'. Together with the other family members present, take your chosen item of food from the plate and pop it in your mouth and eat it, still with no eye contact. You must do this naturally, there must be no "Yum, yum, yum, this is the best grape I've ever had." It is vital also that there should be no teasing with food. Act as if you were cooking and just wanted to test the seasoning. As soon as you have finished your nibble, place your dog's food on the floor in the usual place and walk away without any speech. Remember to stay in the room - you need to see what your dog does without crowding him. The signal you are giving him is, "We've been out hunting. We've killed Mr Tesco (other Supermarkets are available), and we've brought his body back in these carrier bags! The remainder of the kill is in this bowl, but the prime cuts are these grapes or pieces of biscuit that we the leaders have already eaten. This is what is left for you. Fill your boots." Your dog will do one of four things. He can only do one of four things:

1) Go straight to his bowl and eat everything i.e. 'wolf it down', and this is the ideal. If danger now threatens and he has to leave the area he has food in his belly which will improve his survival odds. Dogs are also designed to take their food by bolting it down. They are not designed to graze.

2) It may be that when you put the bowl down your dog just glances at it and walks away as if to say, "Whatever." The signal he is giving is 'Leave it there. When I want to then I'll eat, because the Alpha eats when he likes, as much as he likes'.

3) He may go to his bowl, eat a mouthful or two and then walk away. This option is very similar to option 2. He wants a food bowl down as a status symbol but is also a bit hungry so has a quick snack first.

4) This behaviour is a slightly more unusual...in which the dog takes food from the bowl, takes it to where the humans are and drops it on the

floor in front of them and then eats while trying to make eye contact. An even more extreme version of this behaviour can be displayed by dogs that fill their cheek pouches in the manner of a hamster. They then get right in the humans face and eat. They can go around a whole family putting them in their place in this way. "You're not eating? I am. Or you? Or you? So, let's get this right…none of you are eating and I am? And the Leader has the power of food? Okay, I get it."

If he takes any option other than 1 then, as soon as he deserts his bowl, pick it up at once and throw away the unfinished food. He must not get fed until the next mealtime (that includes food rewards). Will he be hungry? Yes. Will he die? No. Will he have learnt a huge lesson? Oh yes. Even if he has used option 1 and emptied his bowl, it still needs to be removed, cleaned and put out of sight. Even an empty food bowl can be used as a status symbol - "that's where I've trained my humans to deliver my food." Fresh water of course should be available at all times. Do not incorporate this method of Priority Feeding into your normal meal-time as your dog will learn to beg and it is too long winded a process to give a short informative message. Some people will remove the food and save it for later, on the grounds that it's a waste of money to discard it. Dogs are not stupid. They know where their food is kept and where it is thrown away. When the food is removed to the bin this sends a very strong message to your dog - if it had eaten as it should, then the food would be gone anyway. I liken it to little Jimmy who breaks his neighbours window with a catapult. Dad says, "I'm going to throw this away!" Then he puts it on a high shelf. What signal does this give the child? When Dad's calmed down I'll get my catapult back. If however Dad says, "Is this what's just cost me a load of money?" And then snaps the catapult in two and throws it in the bin. Little Jimmy will know that his behaviour is not acceptable.

If your dog attempts to help load the dishwasher or beg or steal from the table then push him away at right angles. If he persists then exclude him for ten seconds of quiet. As leaders you have the absolute right to the pick of the kill.

Have you been told that to show you are the master you must enforce strict control at feeding times? Should you make your dog 'sit', or tell him to 'wait' or 'give a paw' before giving him permission to eat? No, definitely not. This is a human perception of control and when it comes to humans and 'lesser species', we do love to be in control, don't we? Ladies, try this one on your husband or significant other. One weekend when he has had a very stressful period at work lovingly prepare his favourite meal. Tell him to sit at the dining table, pour him a glass of wine and bring in this beautifully cooked and presented meal. Carefully place the meal in front of him wait for him to pick up his knife and fork and just as he is about to cut into his steak say, "WAIT" in a very firm voice. Keep him waiting thirty seconds or so then give him permission to eat. To really show 'girl power' you could remove his meal completely when he's only half way through - that would make him respect you, wouldn't it? On Monday morning he'll leave for work early so that he can call into a divorce lawyer on the way!

Some dogs are 'food aggressive' or have other serious problems around feeding. They may have been a rescue dog that previously had to fight for every mouthful. You may never know the reason that they act this way. It doesn't matter, you can make it better from this point on. With most food issues all will be resolved if you follow the Priority Feeding system detailed above. However we always need a 'plan B' for those times where 'plan A' doesn't work. The following technique rarely has to be used but when it is it sends an incredibly powerful message to the dog.

Enhanced Priority Feeding

Feed the same amount as usual but split the food into three bowls. As with normal priority feeding, before you place the food bowl down you have your grape or biscuit. You only eat before the first food bowl. Put the first bowl down and walk away. As soon as that bowl is empty put down bowl two some distance away and walk away picking up empty bowl one. When the dog has emptied bowl two then bowl three goes down immediately, probably where you placed bowl one. You are not making a big deal of this but staying calm and displaying leadership skills. You've eaten first and then shown in a calm unhurried way you have the power of food. As in "Now I've eaten it's your turn. Here's some food. And some more. Oh and some more. You don't need to get nasty over food because I, the leader, will keep you supplied. I'll look after you. Stick with me kid and you'll be alright." You will be taking all the stress away from your dog and showing that you care...the pack is safe with you.

When to Stop Priority Feeding and Enhanced Priority Feeding

Think of a child being taught to say, "please" or "thank you". Every time they are given something they get a verbal prompt by the adult...'please', 'thank you' or 'ta' followed by praise when they get it right. Once the child has learnt that good manners are appropriate the adult does not have to keep the mantra going. There will however come that day when you give the child a biscuit and they take it without any thanks. The adult then reminds the child by saying something like "Haven't we forgotten to say something?" This should bring the child back into line. If they are a bit more bolshie then the adults may have return to reminding with verbal prompts for a few days.

With a dog you are showing them that there are ground rules. You do this by implementing all of the five elements. With food you are showing that you have complete control over it, when it is distributed and to whom. In the early days (two to three weeks) use Priority Feeding. The dog will also be subjected to the other four elements and the owners status will be enhanced with every new signal.

Once the dog has relinquished leadership, they accept that the 'power of food' is with the owner, therefore, if the leader decides that today he/she doesn't want a biscuit before feeding Fang, that's their choice. The rest of the feeding process stays the same: no speech or eye contact, bowl down, move away, dog deserts bowl, bowl removed at once.

The benefit of stopping Priority Feeding after a short time is that you can keep it in reserve. If a little way down the line the dog decides to test a little bit or perhaps if the owner has been unwell and is not present at mealtimes for a while, it can be re-introduced for maybe a week as well as ensuring they tighten up the other four areas. This is canine "Haven't we forgotten to say something?" The dog will be reminded of the ground rules and should just fall back into place.

If it is necessary to use "Enhanced Priority Feeding" with a dog it is only used until the dog gets the message. It is then replaced with standard Priority Feeding in the normal way.

Bones

The use of bones and rawhide chews can be a cause for concern as it is a means of dogs having access to food at any time. Many dogs will use such treats to 'priority eat' either to humans or other dogs in the pack and thereby claim enhanced status. Bones can also leave owners with large vet bills caused by inter-pack fighting over a food source, bone splinters in the throat, the intestines, the stomach and can sometimes lead to constipation. Incidents related to dogs being given bones or by owners throwing sticks for their dogs can be life threatening and can require surgery. Dental cleaning chews and similar products are fine because they eat those at once and don't keep them as trophies to be flaunted. Remember there is no such thing as a free meal. Don't give dogs treats for no reason, they must earn them. If, for example, you call her across the room and get her to 'sit', that's fine. She's earned it then, she's pleased the boss - movement is subordination. You've called her, she's come and you win.

2) <u>DANGER</u>

When a dog is threatened, frightened or just plain hacked off! they don't call their lawyers. They growl and bite. That's what they do. It's natural, unless you've shown them by your actions that they can trust you to make all the decisions. In their natural state it is the job of the subordinate pack members to guard and then to alert the leaders, the brains of the outfit, who will then decide what to do about it. Often in our confused world the family dog tries to take on both roles. It doesn't work.

Once alerted to a potential threat the leaders assess the situation and decide on a course of action that will best ensure the safety of the pack. They will base this decision on the 'three F's'...Flight, Freeze, Fight. There is some debate over the order these options are selected. Most agree that Fight is the last option. In our opinion the other two are interchangeable depending on the individual circumstances.

'Flight' does not mean running away screaming like a little girl. It is used when the leader decides that if it's going to get dangerous here, if we're not here when it happens then it doesn't matter. He will then lead the pack to safety in a direction of his choosing. There will be no discussion or dissent from the rest of the pack. A big difference between us and the free living canine is that they are not weighed down by possessions. When they leave their rendezvous area for a place of safety they are only leaving ground. Once the danger has passed they can return and carry on as normal. We humans would be leaving buildings, possessions and memories and so might be more inclined to make a stand and risk death and injury. To a canine a flat screen TV and photograph album are not worth dying for.

'Freeze' covers a variety of scenarios from 'That's dangerous, but there's no way to move without being noticed. Don't anyone move a muscle.' to 'It's nothing to do with us, don't get involved.' Or 'They're not coming our way so they're no threat. Keep an eye on them and alert me to any changes in case I have to amend my decision.'

'Fight' is self-explanatory and an option rarely used in the wild. Packs have their own very clearly defined territories and will generally respect those boundaries. There aren't a lot of vets in the wild so an animal that gets in a real fight will be seriously hurt where death is a strong possibility. There are instances of conflict, fighting over better hunting areas or 'mate theft', but generally they will avoid unnecessary confrontation. In our world fights among our canines are much more common. We live in close proximity to each other and unless you are very lucky you won't have a large area of land for the exclusive use of your dog. We get around this by having parks or common land. When you take your dog to the park he may be confused. Is it his territory, or the Labradors from next door, or the vicar's Jack Russell, or any of the multitude of other dogs that share this space? Confused? I should say so. One wrong body posture or eye contact and it's game on.

Should I stay and fight or...?

As you can see, making the right decision is vital to the survival of the pack. It must be you that makes that call that leads to the best outcome. Your dog will respect you and your decisions and in all situations will look to you for guidance. You must not let him down. The first place that you will have to make these decisions on a regular basis is at home.

When anyone knocks on your front door, they want to speak to someone in the house, either a named individual because they are a friend or have business with that person or, because they want to speak to 'Mr and Mrs…The Occupier', because they want to sell you double glazing, talk about religion or ask you to vote for them. In essence you will have two types of callers, those you will invite into your home and those that you will deal with on the doorstep. You will not know what category you are dealing with until you open that door.

The doorbell rings…potential danger…so your dog barks or indicates to you in some other way. In how many homes when the dog barks at the door is the human response a shouted "SHUT UP!" This is a dog we're dealing with here with a limited command of English, so when we respond to being told that danger is approaching the den by roaring we either tell the dog that we're frightened and that it's his job to make the bogeyman go away, or that we are barking to back him up. Now he feels more confident as he shouts through the door, "There's two of us here now so you'd better really back off!" It is the leader's responsibility to assess the level of potential danger, not the dog's. Remember when you were a little child playing in your house with your mother in the back garden hanging the washing out. You see someone coming up your front path. You can't deal with the caller…you're only four…so you call out, "Mum, there's someone at the door." It's unlikely that your mother's response would be to shout and tell you to shut up. It would probably be more along the lines of "Thank you love.

That will be the milkman. I've got to pay him. You carry on playing and I'll deal with it." You're happy, you informed the responsible person and they are dealing with it. You can relax. Use exactly the same rationale with your dog. He's told you of a potential danger. Thank him in a calm, warm voice for doing his job and then deal with the visitor. We do mean use the words 'Thank you'. This becomes a very useful phrase which the dog comes to recognise in a variety of situations inside and out as 'I'm dealing with it. Everything is under control'. Do not allow him to either greet visitors at the door or accompany you when you see guests off the property. By removing him to a different room or area, using a food reward if needed, after you've thanked him and before you open the front door you will be reminding him that you are the decision maker. If the visitor is to be invited in, explain the no speech/eye contact rule to them and ask them to walk straight in and sit down. Remind them that although your dog is cute they have (you hope) come to visit you. Explain to them that they will be able to interact with him in a few minutes once he has shown good manners. You will tell your guests when it is OK to call him. If he approaches your guest before that time then you must deal with it appropriately (as described in more detail in 'The Three Levels of Discipline' outlined shortly).

If you are dealing with the visitor at the door, the salesman, the missionary or political canvasser, deal with them in the normal way except that these people often want to give you a leaflet or brochure which most householders refuse. For the first few weeks of implementing PURE Dog Listening accept any leaflet and deal your caller swiftly. Once they have gone then allow your dog access to the hall so that he can sniff around the front door. He will see you calm and in control reading a double glazing brochure or similar and you will have shown that you can deal with things without a permanent bodyguard.

This will give you complete control. He will have got into the routine of barking, being thanked and moving without any fuss to another room. You will be able to manage every situation. If your visitor is frightened of dogs you will not have to worry about hanging on to your dog while playing 'musical rooms' - you will already be in control, so you can keep your pulse rate down. If you have a child visiting who you do not trust to behave correctly, once again you have no problem. Dog and child do not have to come into contact/conflict. Your pulse rate stays down and as a result so does your dog's.

If the dogs are in the garden and bark at something or if there is noise from a delivery vehicle at the front and they bark at that, thank them in a light warm voice. You are telling them that it's nothing to worry about. If they bark again they are telling you that this needs to be checked by an alpha. Go to where they are indicating. Overact to show them that you are taking their concerns seriously. Thank again in a warm voice and call them to you. You have decided that it's okay for the neighbours to use their garden or have a new washing machine delivered, a 'Freeze' situation. If they bark at the same person/dog/object/post after that then isolate for a short while (because they are questioning your decision) until they stop barking. Immediately he stops then let him out, if he barks again then silently put him into isolation again, when he is quiet he is let back out - if he remains quiet, then he can stay...that is his reward.

Beware the self styled 'dog expert' guest who does not follow instructions - the type who goes straight into a dog's personal space despite all the signals the dog is giving and then is surprised when he (it's usually a man) gets bitten. If a guest refuses to help you resolve your problems I suggest you keep human and dog apart. If a visitor to a house with children was asked not to give the children sweets because they were undergoing dental treatment, very few people would hand over a big bag of sweets to them saying, "Don't take any notice of what your mum and dad say, eat up." Yet people don't think twice about interfering with dogs against the owners wishes. Remember, the person who ignores your request will often be the first person to complain when they get bitten.

Outside the home, you, the leader must be the one to decide whether to use 'Freeze', 'Flight' or 'Fight'. If you see or hear something ahead that you don't like or you think might frighten or annoy your dog, just deviate from your intended route without any drama and he will come with you. Problem solved, before it becomes a problem. If he notices something before you (it may be a sound or smell and not in your range of senses), as soon as you pick up on his often subtle indications thank him, reassess the area and take the appropriate action.

This may just mean crossing the road to avoid confrontation, stepping back into a driveway because of skate-boarders on the pavement or may involve no action at all. You will be saying to him "Thanks for that but I've already got it in hand."

High stress = lower ability to learn

Low stress = higher ability to learn

The 'Calm Hold'

Can you think clearly and logically when in a state of panic? Of course not, it is as if your brain was filled with cotton wool. You make irrational decisions or no decisions at all. You only have to look at the television news on most nights to see examples of this behaviour…war, natural disasters such as earthquakes, or ones with a human element such as a train crash or a football stadium stampede. If we, who are supposedly the most intelligent creatures and have some knowledge of what's happening can't hold it together, what hope has a dog when facing their first exposure to fireworks for example?

To deal with any nervous reaction, obsessive

behaviour or to just give a dog time to think and moderate their behaviour, use the 'Calm Hold': take the dog by the collar and draw them to you and hold them firmly but not roughly at your side. No speech and no eye contact. At first they will continue to shake, attempt to chase their tail, bark or perform some other undesirable behaviour. As they realise that you are relaxed and your pulse rate low they will ask themselves the question: 'Why am I doing this?' They will then gradually relax and you will be able to release them, again with no speech or eye contact. Be prepared to repeat if required. Each time you use the 'Calm Hold' the time taken for the dog to relax will decrease. It takes as long as it takes. Every dog is an individual. When dealing with a problem that will last for sometime, such as on Bonfire Night it is useful to have a pile of magazines to hand and to sit on the floor looking through them. This makes it more comfortable for you if you have to hold the dog for long periods. It also makes you appear more relaxed.

3) THE WALK (Follow my leader)

Who decides where and for how long you go for?

Before you start the walk it is vital that you and your dog are relaxed - as a result you will be in control. The moment you lose that feeling go back to the area where it was all fine, revise and go forward, try this a couple of times and if no progress is made then call the walk off (consequences of actions) and try again later.

First and foremost, you will have to desensitise your dog to all the triggers that make him explode prior to the walk. We want your dog to look excited but with self control. Both human and canine must be in a calm state before the walk begins. So get into the habit of having the lead out and about - just because the lead is in view it doesn't mean you're off on a walk - you may want to clean it or put it around your neck as the next fashion accessory! If your dog goes over-the-top when you put your wellies on, for example, then put them on, disregard the dog and have a cuppa and when the dog is calm then call your dog over and put the lead on and start your walk.

Lots of short practice walks in a day are better than doing one long one and getting it wrong. Your short ones gradually become longer as the days go by and before you know it you'll be off around the countryside having a lovely time together. When we mean short, to begin with you'll be doing probably 5 minutes, 5 or 6 times a day. As the time increases then the number of times decrease. Short-term pain for you in exchange for a long-term gain for all. If your dog throws a paddy because you have changed your routine and the attitude of "We go out now!" and starts to ping around the house, please remember it is because you have now changed and you make the decision of where and when you go out. For his part he will try in many ways to get you to do what you always do. It is not because he hasn't had a huge run. We have all seen a child 'performing' in a toy or sweet shop when they don't get what they want - if the adult gives in then the child will know that they can always get their way by using certain behaviours. If the adult stands firm then a lesson is learned and life gets a lot more pleasant for all. The same is true of dogs: get the lesson in early.

We have to educate his mind on how to fit in with us and if you give in on poor behaviour, he realises that he can wind you around his little paw. Yes, dogs do need exercise and you *will* get on your long walks again, but its best to leave these for when all is fine and dandy - there are lots of team building games you can play in the house and garden to enhance your bond and your dog will love them and get the physical exercise (and education) he needs too.

You can make teaching walking to heel into a game of 'follow my leader', have fun with it and your dog will enjoy it too - don't walk around like a stick insect demanding attention, get good heel work by being fun, interesting, not demanding.

Remember that in the wild, no group-living canine ever just goes 'for a walk'. You would be well advised to really get things right at home first so that when you do go 'on the hunt' you will be in control. You will be presenting your dog with a blank canvas, a chance to hear four of the five messages clearly. A chance to understand the world from a different perspective, without responsibilities and with full permission to just be a dog. By implementing Dog Listening in its PUREst form, as the dogs would do themselves, we're saying, "We know what's important to you and we'll show you that you can trust us. Then we'll show you a world where you can just live life to the full."

If you can resist the temptation to take your dog out into the big wide world before they are ready and convince him to really believe that you can be trusted to make all the right decisions, then you will reap the benefits. However, we know that all sorts of pressures can be brought to bear on you. Preconceived ideas like 'you must walk your dog for an hour in the morning and again at night' are common. This advice is sometimes given whatever the size or age of dog, the family make-up or home conditions. If you live in a busy urban environment and your dog's walk is around the block on a lead with his nose level with the exhaust pipes of passing vehicles, is it good for him? Ten minutes structured play in the garden is worth an hour plodding around the block on the lead. We have suggested some games in the 'Team Building' chapter which utilise dogs' natural instincts and so provide exercise for both mind and body. Use your garden well - it's an oft neglected tool in bonding with a dog. We appreciate that we live in the real world and that not everybody has a dog-proof garden or indeed any garden. In such cases of course you have to take your dog outside if only for toileting purposes. If you fall into this category then it is even more important that you consistently give your dog the right signals and that you have a plan in your head as to what you will do if the situation changes. If you stand hopping from one foot to another not knowing what to do your dog's reaction will be

'Lead, Follow or Get Out Of The Way!' The leader knows everything and cannot be wrong so 'Umm' is not a decision, it's the first sign of panic.

Who leads the walk, decides where to go and how long it lasts? The leader. Therefore, when you leave the house, all humans go through the front door first. Your dog on his lead so he knows he's going out. No speech or eye contact is required. Open the door a little but not wide enough to get a dog's nose in. If he tries to push through or makes any forward movement then silently close door. Wait 5/10 seconds and repeat. The message you are giving is 'I can stand here all day. I'm in no rush and therefore you will not make me angry or upset me in any other way'. He will realise that if he is going to get a walk, then he has to let you out first and will physically step back from the door to let the leader (you) have priority. Usually with one dog this takes about 5 or 6 goes but if you have a strong willed dog it will take as long as it takes. If however he decides he will barge on by, then close the door so that you are separated, and after five seconds open it again and 9/10 times your dog will walk back in - if he does not you walk away and the dog follows as he is on a lead, reward at your side and try again. He should be on a lead even if you are only going to your car. When you get to your destination he should only come out of the car on the lead even if you are on the common. Walk a short distance from the car (ten or fifteen yards is fine) before release him. This reminds him that you are the decision maker, not him, and that today you have decided that the walk will start from...here.

If you are not happy letting your dog off the lead then refer to the 'Recall' section later in this book.

To improve the recall once you do have it well established, use a happy *light* voice 'come', open your arms in a welcoming manner and gradually bring your hands together across your lap as he comes to you. Should he hesitate move back a few paces with an encouraging, "Come! Come! Come!" (a bit of Michael Jackson moon walking generally helps too!) Remember, everything revolves around consequences of actions. Particularly in the early stages he will be thinking: 'What's in this for me?' so when he comes when called reward him with whatever works for him as an individual. It may be just a little fuss, a game or a small treat. If it works, use it. If he ignores the command just turn on your heel and walk away briskly, he will not want to be out of favour with the Team Leaders: exclusion from the pack is the ultimate punishment which he will do anything to avoid.

Heel-work: We like to call this 'Follow my Leader' because it does what is says on the tin. Remember, you are the Team leader and you decide when and where you go. This can be taught as a fun exercise rather than boring your dog witless or with long periods of obedience training using compulsion. Practice fun multi-directional walking with the odd stop indoors and in the garden, both on and off the lead. Walk four or five paces and if you find a piece of furniture in your way then turn left, right or about-turn. When you find yourself facing a wall then again turn left, right, about-turn or maybe you might jog backwards for two or three paces. Unpredictability and fun is the name of the game. If at any time during the walk his behaviour is unacceptable, try three times to regain control with gentle change of direction or 'Calm Hold'. If you're practising outdoors, apply the same method and if you find that you're experiencing difficulties simply turn around without a word and return to the house, remove the lead and put it away. The walk ends and he gets at least half an hour of the cold shoulder treatment. He will soon learn consequences of actions.

When we deal with clients who have problems with their dogs showing aggression to other dogs while on the walk, we often find that their life is no longer their own. They join the 'Early Morning Club' taking their dogs for a walk at five in the morning to avoid confrontation. There are problems with this, not only are you permanently tired but who are you going to meet at that time of the morning? Fellow club members with aggressive dogs. So now, if there is confrontation it won't just be "your mother was a hamster and your father smelt of elderberries,"...a full-blown bloodbath might be more likely. When these owners leave home at anytime with their dog they just know that it will be a disaster and of course it will, a self-fulfilling prophecy. Stress levels are already high before leaving the house so the dog is on the alert. Then what happens? Wouldn't you just know it? It's a plot! Someone is coming towards you with the very breed of dog that your dog hates. Your blood pressure shoots through the roof and just in case your dog hadn't noticed, you shorten the lead so he can't breathe. Dogs are very perceptive so he'll probably think: 'Somethings up. Something or someone is frightening my human. The very human that I'm duty bound to protect'. He looks around and what does he see? The approaching dog, the thing causing upset to the human. The only option is to see this threat off, so your dog pulls, barks and snarls. You get embarrassed, frightened or angry. The owner of the other dog either gets angry as well and tells you to keep your dog under control even if their dog is just as aggressive, or maybe they just look disapproving - either way you feel bad.

What can you do to make the situation better? Let's take the uncertainty and embarrassment away. Consider the use of 'stooges' - make enquiries of your friends and acquaintances to find people who have dogs and would be prepared to help you. The two things you worry about most are meeting another dog (so lets make that happen in controlled conditions) and the disapproval of the other dog owner. If they are working with you then that won't happen. Arrange with your stooge - mobile phones are great for this - to be at a particular junction and as you are walking with your dog on the left footpath, they come around the corner on the right footpath. By coming across other dogs in pre-arranged locations and situations you will ensure that you're 'happy and in control'. Even if your dog barks or shows aggression to the other dog just thank him and keep walking. You won't need to get embarrassed because the other dog owner will be expecting him to bark and will ignore the behaviour.

Repeat the passes with a friendly verbal greeting ("Sorry about that, he's in training...") to the other dog owner. No matter what your dog is doing, just keep moving, you decide where you're going. Carry on walking for 25 yards or so then both turn around and repeat. Your dog will get a little confused now because previously you'd always lost credibility in this situation but now you're cool. If you're lucky you may be able to set up two or three stooges along your walk and this would really drive the point home that you are relaxed and confident. Take your time, don't be rushed and pushed into a rigid timetable. It takes as long as it takes. Once your dog realises that you don't get stressed at the sight of another dog he'll know that he doesn't need to look after you and can relax.

Another option you can use, particularly if you find this is not helping or you're not confident enough to pass a dog or person, is to walk away at a right angle to the other side of the road. Depending on how your dog is and how you feel, you may like to continue to walk past the danger or return in the direction you came. In the early stages if this is too much for your dog simply walk back home – your dog will appreciate your decision. As you progress then you can do this exercise with a stooge maybe a little further from home, still keeping home in sight. Each time you turn away from the danger and walk towards home the more confident your dog will become in your decisions until you get to a stage that your dog trusts you simply to walk past on the other side of the road of what used to be an issue. The next stage will be to pass by a danger on the same side of the road when you are confident that your dog has blanked the dog's or person's approach. Be light hearted and lead by example with a calm and an authoritative manner. Ensure you pass by closest to the problem keeping your dog on the other side of you: you are the ultimate protector.

If you were walking with your child hand in hand and something ahead didn't look right, you'd do just the same, without a word. Your child would not have picked up on any stress as you made nothing of it. If there was something ahead that bothered your child or Granny then, crossing the road or walking away would be a natural thing for you to do, you are not showing them you're a wimp, you're showing them that you will take care of them - that this decision is the right one to take right now.

It is a good idea to maybe pre-empt your dog's reaction and take evasive action even before your dog has reacted - as we've noted already, humans can be proactive where dogs are only reactive in situations they are unsure of. If you can make an assertive decision, then your dog will become confident with your abilities to take the right action in times of doubt. This will mean, as you continue, your dog will look to you to take the lead.

During the walk call him back to you at irregular intervals, place him on a lead, try a small amount of heel-work or just walk on the lead for twenty yards or so with him then make a big fuss of him and release him again. This will make training both fun and teach him that being put on a lead does not always mean the end of the walk. Keep the walk interesting. Don't always take the same route, alter your pace, turn left, turn right, stop, run backwards. Keep him guessing, "Where are we going now? What are we going to do?" Walk with a swagger - remember 'Del boy' and you'll be his 'most favourite'. Don't forget to turn a different way occasionally on leaving home just to keep him guessing, even walking the usual route but on the opposite pavement to normal will keep him on his toes.

4) REJOINING AND AFFECTION

This is the area that causes humans the most problems because we, in our day to day lives, continually make eye contact and talk to one another. We use eye contact to show that we can be trusted, that we are interested in the other person's point of view or to show affection towards that person. Lack of eye contact is considered rude in our culture. Dogs use eye contact in a wholly different manner: a senior canine does not make eye contact with a subordinate until he wants to interact with them. When that interaction is complete eye contact is broken. In using the following techniques you will not be either rude or cruel, quite the opposite, you will be showing that you are a strong, caring, credible leader who will put the safety of the pack and its members before anything else. This does not require you to act like a drill sergeant - by using the right techniques a slightly built female can achieve better results than a body-builder type.

Rejoining takes place countless times a day. Anytime you leave your dog for any reason they will, on your return, go through a series of rituals to check if the leadership and thus the whole pack dynamic has changed. While they are going through the ritual, attempting to gain attention, it is vital that you give them **no cues, either verbally or by eye or physical contact**. If they jump up in your face or try to climb onto your lap for attention just firmly push them away, again with no cues of any kind. Once they realise that their pestering won't work they will lay down as if sulking. What they are actually doing is trying to work out what has changed. Leave them for at least five minutes after they have settled. When *you* are ready, call your dog to you for a fuss. If they become demanding or over excited just revert to blanking them until they learn manners and understand 'personal space'. If your dog does not modify their behaviour take them by the collar and *firmly and silently* remove them from the room and exclude them from the pack. If they decide that they are not going to let you take hold of them without turning it into a game of 'chase' around the room, do not get stressed but just leave the room yourself and close the door behind you. It doesn't matter what you do - go to the kitchen and have a cup of tea, go and have a lie down. The important thing is that the dog will not have got their way and they will have lost the pack.

To prevent a dog using their small size, speed or agility to evade consequences or tease their human you can permanently attach a 'home training/ trailing line' to your dog's collar for use around the house and garden in the initial training period. The line is very light and quite long and attaches to the collar by a conventional but light clip. It should not be left on if you go out and leave the dog home alone. The line just trails behind the dog and does not have a hand loop - this is to prevent snagging on furniture. Should it get dirty it can go in the washing machine. Because the line is so light most dogs soon forget that it's even there. It doesn't matter what the dog does, hide under the furniture for example - simply take hold of the line and remove them from their hiding place. If he tries to run around the room, stand on the line and stop him. You now have control at all times.

When he has learnt consequences of actions allow him to rejoin the pack but ensure he has five minutes back in your company before you call him to you. Particularly in the early stages when you call a dog to you after the five minute break it is important that you a) make eye contact and b) call them to you using their name and simple commands like, "Spot, Come." The moment he comes to you say, "Good dog." Gently stroke his head and the back of the neck at the same time.

The invitation to 'approach the throne' should be pleasurable for a dog. Not a stare and barked command. Approach this as if you were welcoming your best friend. If they ignore the invitation, and they might at first, as they sense a change in the balance of power, don't get upset, raise your voice, go to them or keep calling them. If they ignore you it will be to test your leadership skills. Leaders in a canine world don't lose their tempers or plead with subordinates. If they blank you then they need to know they've blown it. They were given the chance to interact with you and blew it. You now blank them until you decide to call them again. You'll see a much quicker response next time.

Everything is done on **your terms, not the dog's**.

Discipline

In every group there must be discipline in some form so that the group can function smoothly. It doesn't matter whether in the family, workplace, sports field or just in our day to day dealings with other people. Discipline is a set of rules written or unwritten, the most effective form is self-discipline. Often when humans think of discipline, enforcement is top of their list of options. The first tool at your disposal when talking about enforcing your will on a dog is physical force, either hitting, shaking, or shouting. Please don't waste your time. Apart from the fact that it is cruel it just doesn't work. If you hit or use any other form of violence on a dog such as 'electric shock' or 'spiked prong' collars there will only be one of two outcomes. You will either crush the dog's spirit or he will bite you. I think you'll agree…not the result you want to achieve.

We do need ground rules, but rather than use the 'Don't ask him. Tell him!' or 'Just make him do it!'

method, we prefer to use 'Appropriate Correction'. Why? Because we are kind, considerate, warm human beings. Oh! And because it works much better than anything else we've found. If you constantly nag and witter at your dog even if you're not telling him off but just telling him your plans for the day then you are setting up a 'wall of sound' or 'white noise' and your dog will think: 'He's going off on one again' and will switch off. If you then need to interact with him about something important you shouldn't be surprised if he takes no notice. If you use the method of PURE Dog Listening as detailed in this book, when you say your dog's name you will get an immediate and positive response rather than "Talk to the paw."

The Three Levels of Discipline

1) To be applied when a dog is nudging or otherwise demanding attention. Without looking or talking to your dog firmly push him away. Do not do this roughly but rather as if you were pulling back a very heavy set of curtains.

When would you use this technique? As we mentioned in the 'Rejoining' section when you or other pack members return home in the early stages you may be mugged by the family dogs demanding attention. Once they have learnt (by you giving the correct signals during rejoining) that every action has a consequence they will become much more respectful of your status and personal space. This means that they will still come to greet you on your return but will not leap all over you, because they now know that if they give you time and personal space to take your coat off or do anything else you need to do then you will be in a position to interact with them much sooner. A well mannered dog who wants attention from you will 'just happen' to be in your eye line looking cute. They are giving you non verbal signals that they are respectful and available should you wish to invite them to approach 'the throne'. If you want to invite your dog then make warm eye contact and call him to you as detailed earlier. If however you don't want interaction at that time, perhaps you have a phone call to make, then just break eye contact and the message that you are busy will be received loud and clear. As your leadership is established the amount of respect you will be given will increase but things can slip. We teach children to say, "please" and "thank" you and not to interrupt adult conversation but sometimes they forget. You give a biscuit and they wander off without a word, you then have to remind them of their manners. The same applies to dogs. They will learn how to behave but sometimes will forget themselves and just approach you and give you a nudge, usually when you're holding a cup of hot coffee saying, "Give me a fuss." Just push him away because if you talk to him he's won. Give him the correct information then he will be reminded that he has to wait to be invited.

2) To be applied in cases of minor infractions (similar to when you would say to a child "Don't do that love."). Take the dog by the collar and move them through at least 90 degrees (180 is even better) away from the area of interest. If they repeat

the behaviour you move them again. Three strikes and they're out. You have to up the ante.

This is for those occasions when your dog is doing something that you don't want him to but it's not a big deal. This is important because if you do overreact and make a big deal of it then your dog knows how to press your buttons when he wants a reaction from you. Imagine that you are sitting with friends and family one evening chatting or watching TV. Someone has a packet of crisps and puts the empty wrapper in the bin in the lounge. It's food and a senior pack member has left some. None of the other high ranking members are interested in it so in your dog's eyes it would be stupid not to at least check it out. He sticks his head in the bin and the sky falls in "No! Leave! Bad dog!" The dog doesn't know what all the drama is about but will store the information for future use. Next time a similar situation arises he'll use it against you, one minute you'll be having a pleasant evening and the next the waste bin will go flying across the room. The dog won't worry about you shouting at him. He now has control. Everyone in the room has stopped talking, reading or watching TV and is paying attention to him. The dog is the centre of attention, result!

Instead of shouting and losing control try acting like a leader. Calmly and silently move him and he will soon realise that there is no benefit in his behaviour. You can use this in a variety of situations - the dog that stands and puts their paws on the window ledge to be a nosey neighbour, the dog that climbs on the furniture uninvited, the list is endless. If you don't like the behaviour whatever it is then calmly interrupt it.

3) To be applied when a behaviour is unacceptable, which includes all aggression and anything that you respond to by thinking: 'I'm not putting up with that!' Take the dog by the collar and remove them from the room into isolation, short and sweet. Each time they repeat the behaviour you extend the isolation period.

You would use this with a dog that didn't take the hint from any previous measures. For other more serious offences you would go straight in at this level. Mouthing, biting, aggressive displays are a complete 'No-No' but remember that you set the ground rules and decide what you will or will not accept.

All three of the above responses must be applied using no speech and no eye contact.

If you act silently and instantly the dog will make the connection: 'Every time I perform behaviour X I get isolated. I lose the pack. I crave the safety and companionship of the pack. What would happen if I didn't do X?' The answer is that if the dog changes his behaviour of his own free will then he will be rewarded by being allowed to stay with the pack which is his main aim.

If you talk to and look at the dog during the isolation process you will confuse him and deflect his attention from his actions. The probability is that he would repeat the offending behaviour on his return.

I was given a very vivid example of how speaking can confuse a dog when I had two clients with the same major problem on consecutive days. Note I said 'major' problem. Often we are contacted by clients they tell us they have a problem, just the one. Aggression, not recalling, fouling in the house etc. I have yet to deal with a dog that has only one problem. That 'one' is usually a symptom of deeper underlying issues. The 'problem' that these two clients presented with was toe biting. This is quite a common behaviour which covers a mild 'tickling' action, through 'irritating'...to downright painful.

The first client's dog had started at 'tickling' but had moved to 'irritating'. Usually what happens is that the family are sitting around in the evening with bare or stockinged feet. The dog approaches and sniffs, licks or gently nibbles toes. The recipient of the pedicure giggles or pulls their feet away with a laugh. What a good game. Then the human alternates the foot and gives further attention to the dog who now knows how to get his humans dancing, even when they're sitting down. Other family members laugh, which encourages the dog who then decides that he'll do it to everybody. When they can't concentrate on what they're doing due to the nibbling, people can suffer a severe sense of humour failure. Now this dog was a nice little fellow but persistent was his middle name. We tried moving him away as in level 2 above but to no avail.

He nipped the husband's right foot and was isolated. He came back in waited a very short while and nipped the left foot. Out he went again. On his return he looked at the husband gave him a wide berth and nipped the wife's right foot. Isolation number three. When he returned you could almost hear the cogs in his head going round. He looked at the husband as if to say "I did your right foot and your left foot and both times got isolated." He then looked at the wife. 'I did your right foot and got isolated...so...on the balance of probability if I do your left foot...do you know what? I don't think I'll bother?' Three very short isolations, message learnt.

The second client's dog was on the painful end of the scale. We followed the same procedure and when it became obvious that she wasn't going to take the hint I said to the client, "Next time she does that, straight out. No speech or eye contact." He replied "Got it." She nipped again and I gave the client the nod. He took her by the collar and while leading her from the room said, "Right young lady, out you go. You're a very naughty little girl." I said "No. Don't say anything." He replied "I didn't." His wife said "You did." He got angry and said, "No I didn't." I thought they were going to have a domestic but then his mother-in-law stepped in and said, "You did speak love." For some reason he accepted correction from his out-laws. We tried again, and again but he couldn't stop talking. It took him eleven attempts before he made it to the door in silence. When he came in he said, "I just stopped myself. I bit my tongue to keep myself from speaking. It's not my fault. I'm Welsh you see."

Consider the different messages the two dogs were given. In the first case unacceptable behaviour had an instant consequence. No confusion...a simple message 'Do that and you lose the pack'. The dog was able to moderate his behaviour because he knew what was required. The second had only confusion when being corrected. A wall of sound which blocked any message we were trying to get through. She would return to the room none the wiser and just think: 'Now where was I? Oh yes, toe biting...'. We got there with the second dog but it was hard work.

5) LEADERSHIP THROUGH PLAY

No canine ever goes for a walk in the wild to look for danger and waste energy - they go out to hunt to get food so that the pack survives and also to check boundaries to protect their patch. When they do go out it's only with the authority of the leader. If on leaving the den and travelling two hundred yards a particularly stupid moose steps out in front of the pack then they will kill and eat. They will then return to the den area. They won't think that they should walk for another twenty five miles as part of an aerobic workout! Their aim in leaving the den was to get food and they've achieved that with minimal effort and injury, job done, an efficient use of time and energy.

If they don't complete the equivalent of a marathon everyday what do they do? They sleep and they play. Why do they play? For the same reasons that humans do. For fun, to keep fit, to bond with the pack/team. That is why we have school or pub football teams and why groups of salesman go on paint-balling weekends…to help bond the unit. When dogs play as a group it also helps the younger members hone their hunting abilities and learn a range of skills.

If your dog tries to tease you with a toy with a view to you chasing him, ignore him until he brings the toy right up to you and then, if he is still holding it in his mouth - without grabbing it or making eye contact – simply push him away. If he drops it in your lap take control of it, again with no speech or eye contact. When you have control of the toy put it out of reach. You can, if you want to, initiate a game with the toy after a few minutes because you will be showing that it's *your* decision as leader to play now. Don't leave a large number of toys lying around, just a couple of favourites so he can entertain himself when he's on his own. Any special toys that you use to interact with him should be put away after use and only brought out by you on your terms. Toys are trophies, toys are status and toys are power.

Never play tugging or wrestling games with any dog. These are not 'games' to a dog but a very real battle for supremacy that can easily get out of hand.

Dogs can play as individuals or on a one-to-one basis but the very best games are the organised team building ones which are always initiated by the leader. They mean more, are far more fun and pro-active and remind pack members that they have a strong credible leader.

Teams or groups that relax and have fun together work more efficiently. The family that plays together stays together. This is as true with dogs as with humans.

Here are a few things that you could try. Remember a dog that doesn't play is a dog with too many management decisions to make. Take those away and he will relax, then you can show him how to play and chill.

They love play as we and our children do, but you have to be in the right frame of mind to be able to do just that, play. It is a great tool for learning as well as having fun.

The Game of Fetch

If your dog is big and bouncy then it would be a good idea to start this exercise off when the dog is calm and maybe roll the ball instead of throwing it. If your dog is not an enthusiastic ball/toy player you will have to encourage him by waggling the toy in front of his feet and buzzing him up a bit before you throw.

So your dog doesn't bring it back! Oh no, what do I do now? If he goes off and plays his own game and does not try and involve you in any way, if you are outside walk inside (or vice versa) and more often that not he will drop it and come to see where you have gone!! "Why are you not watching me???" will be the likely reaction. Basically he has lost his audience and you're not begging him to play!! That's a different result than he expected methinks!

With a dog such as this it is ideal to start the game off inside or make an 'alley way' for him, so he can't run off and he has to bring it towards you. When he turns around with the ball in his mouth then turn your body sideways and clap your hands to encourage him. By turning yourself sideways you are not in a challenging position with eye to eye contact (just the odd glance) but if you turn completely away you show yourself as a subordinate or prey. When he does come with the ball, reward and throw again…the games continues. Quit while you are ahead, three is plenty to begin with. Make it happen by putting your most exciting voice on and be really enthusiastic with your body language. For a reserved dog you will not have to be so demonstrative, but be inventive.

If, when the dog comes with the ball and does not release it, offer a swap - a piece of chicken maybe. The next time he goes for the ball he may drop it half way and run for the food reward…oh no, he thinks…forget the ball - I want that chook!! Well, unlucky mate, the deal is you bring me the ball and then you get a reward. No such thing as a free lunch. In this instance go up to the ball and kick it around encouraging him to pick it up and bring it to you.

Chase/Follow My Leader

Make the heel work into a game of follow my leader - run around the garden getting him to chase you and if he jumps up stop and wait until all is calm and then start off again. Sprint, change your direction, walk, change, trot, walk, change etc. with a swagger and a fun tone of voice. If you are having fun you can bet your bottom dollar that he is too.

Try some homemade agility courses by putting some obstacles up to jump over or some cones to weave in and out of and enjoy.

Teaching The Property Search

This is a particularly useful exercise which you can teach and play both in your garden or when out on a walk. Most dogs will love this but some Bull Breeds or Pugs may have problems because of their noses. Even then it's still worth trying even if you have to make the exercise easier for them.

You will need a selection of articles ('tickle' in dog handler's parlance) in varying materials: an old purse, a knotted sock, an old wine cork, for example. Virtually anything except sharp metal will do, so before you throw anything out at home ask yourself, "Could this make a good 'tickle'? If the answer is 'yes' put it in your special 'tickle box' or bag. I wouldn't bother with metal items in the early stages as many dogs won't pick them up. As you are only doing this for fun there's no point in trying to force them. Once you've got the system going well then you could try introducing a set of car keys into the game. Make sure they're old keys in case your dog doesn't find them!

Now to start, you will need an assistant. Half an hour before you go on your walk (or into the garden) ensure that either you or your assistant have the 'tickles' that you are going to use in pockets, carried in the hand or stuffed up jumpers so that they get well impregnated with human scent. Your dog is going to learn to find articles with human scent on them which are alien to the environment that you are searching. When you reach the venue you hold your dog on the lead while your assistant shows them the property that they are going to hide. Ensure that you work into the wind i.e. that the wind from the search area is blowing towards your dog so that they can pick up air scent. If you work with the wind coming from behind you then you will mask the scent of the 'tickles' with your own personal scents.

It is best for the first few attempts to just use one fairly large 'tickle', maybe a purse. The assistant rushes around (at this early stage overacting is not only acceptable but desirable) pretending to put the 'tickle' in two or three places before placing just out of sight perhaps in long grass or behind a small bush. While this is going on you must be encouraging your dog saying excitedly, "What's he doing? What's he got?" The assistant then pretends to put the article in two or three more places and then returns and shows the dog their empty hands. You then run forward with your dog on a lead saying, "Where is it?" Seek and fetch." Most dogs will at first check out the places that the assistant went to first or last until they work their way to the actual hide. As soon as the dog hits the spot and finds the article give huge amounts of praise and call "Fetch". If they hesitate make yourself really fun to be with, run backwards or go into 'Homer Simpson' (whoo-hooo!) mode and you will be irresistible to any dog. It doesn't really matter if they don't retrieve the property direct to your hand at this stage. The point of the exercise is to get them running around, having fun, using their natural instincts and working for, and focusing on, you.

Once the dog has got the hang of searching you can introduce extra items (usually up to four) so that they get used to retrieving several things during a search. Take it in turns with your helper to either hold the dog or place the search articles. Once searching well then you can put property out without the dog seeing. You then sit the dog facing the search area and release them off lead with the command 'Seek and Fetch'. Although this is an exercise with a serious purpose when used by Police dogs searching crime scenes for weapons, stolen property etc., it is still a fun exercise that can be enjoyed by other dogs and handlers too. This is a great bonding tool. The exercise is really a form of non violent hunting. You direct the hunt, the dog relinquishes the 'kill' to you. Hey! You must be a leader!

When your dog really has a good understanding of the exercise you can use it to make the walks more interesting. You go to the woods for a walk and let your dog off lead. He wanders on ahead to check his 'pee mails' and while he is otherwise occupied you can throw several articles into the undergrowth. You continue your walk and let your dog have a good run. On the way back, as you are approaching the place where your dog anticipates being put on the lead, you stop and set him up for a search. Will he like it? You bet. You've turned a routine stroll up the road and walk around the woods into something special.

I (Robin) said at the start of this piece that the property search can be useful and indeed it can. I want to tell you a story.

Many years ago before mobile phones I knew a senior detective whose wife fell in love with my police dog. He approached me and said "I've just had a very unsubtle hint from my wife that she wants a 'surprise present' of a German Shepherd from the same place that you got Acco. I put him in touch with the kennel and he got a really good specimen which I helped him to train. One of the exercises I taught him was property searching. Shortly after training his dog he moved to the Isle of Wight so I didn't see him for a while. Some months later I bumped into him at Headquarters. He was raving about how good his dog was and told me that late one winter's afternoon he had taken his dog for a long walk on Culver Down. This is a very bleak place on the East Wight. There used to be heavy guns there to protect the Solent but they are long since gone although the concrete emplacements remain. There is nothing on the down except a café that is only open in the summer. In the winter the only people to make the long journey to the downs are courting couples as they can tuck their cars out of sight between the bunkers and dog walkers. Martin started his walk at dusk but by the time he got back to his car it was pitch black. He put his hand in his pocket, no keys! As I said, this was before mobile phones so he couldn't phone his wife to bring the spare keys out - he had a torch, but that was locked in the car. He couldn't knock on a car window for help because he would probably been punched on the nose and accused of being a 'peeping Tom'. What to do then? Could the dog do a property search for real rather than as a game?

Of course he could. When training a police dog he doesn't know that he is not finding a murder weapon only that he is searching. He doesn't try less because he's 'only training'. Off Martin went, retracing his steps and after 150 yards there is a jingle in the dark as the dog located and retrieved the keys. Martin realised that he'd pulled a handkerchief from his pocket at that location, obviously catching his keys in so doing and dropping them into long grass.

Be aware that in teaching this exercise you are saying to your dog, "Go out there and bring me back anything with human scent that is alien to the environment." A dog can only be a dog, so you can't say, "Find me a blue handbag, a Nokia mobile phone and a knife." The dog will retrieve anything including the bag, phone and knife. If someone has walked through the search area and after lighting their last cigarette thrown the packet away, then the dog is right to retrieve that as well. Don't tell your dog he's wrong, take the article, praise him and send him back into the search area.

"whys he running away? Thought we were playing"

Although it is not something that many readers of this book will be involved in you can of course refine the search to specific groups of items or odours, food, dry or wet rot, cancers, cash, firearms or the most common: drugs or explosives. Although many of the techniques are similar there are very important differences. We do not want a dog to pick up and puncture a bag full of heroin or cocaine and we really don't want a dog that has located a bomb to retrieve it to us with tail wagging. I can tell you that no matter how fast a dog can run he would, in a case such as this, have a hard job catching up with his handler!

Other Learning Through Play Possibilities

Once you have a solid grounding in your relationship with your dog you may want to get involved in other enjoyable activities. There is no problem with this at all and it can be hugely enjoyable so long as you are careful in your choice. As with choosing a vet, trust your instincts. Do you feel comfortable with these people? If not don't get involved, try elsewhere. Before you take your dog along and sign up, ask if you can just attend on your own and sit in and watch one evening. Any club worth their salt will be happy to agree to attract new members. If they are not happy for you to watch, why not? Decide what sort of club you want to join, do you want to take part in a competitive way or just for fun? Many clubs such as agility cater for both, others are more focused. Remember you are doing this for enjoyment so take your time to find the club and activity that best suits you and your dog.

Agility: great fun and good for fitness in both dog and handler as well as promoting bonding. Do not start this until your dog is at least a year old to avoid damaging joints that are not fully formed.

Obedience classes: Be very selective. The best are very good, the worst are dreadful. Be aware that anyone can hire a church hall and 'teach obedience'. Visit first, watch carefully - do the instructors appear competent? Are the dogs (and their owners) happy or cowed? Be alert for any signs of heavy handed behaviour either physical or emotional. Get an assurance from the instructors that they do not use electric shock or prong (spiked) collars. If they tick all the boxes join and enjoy.

Flyball: a very fast sport, quickly burning off energy but is repetitive and can cause some dogs to be ball obsessed.

Working Dog Trials: This is the pinnacle of recreational dog training and covers a range of skills, obedience, agility, tracking, searching. Any breed of dog can participate and it has a range of skill levels. You can either work your way up or stick at a level that you are comfortable with.

These and many other pastimes are out there for you and your dog. You may however just want to go for a stroll in the park together. Whatever your choice, as long as your dog is in no doubt as to his place in the scheme of things, you will both be happy.

Road Safety

Little doggie
Busy street
Motor car
Mincemeat.

Anon

CHAPTER 7

Understanding common problems people experience with their dogs

As mentioned already, it never matters what your dog does only what you do in response. If you make nothing of something (but be proactive) it will be just that: nothing. BUT, you must be calm, confident, convincing and consistent to make it happen.

What is Abnormal Behaviour?

If your dog displays any behaviour that is not normal for him, such as asking to go out in the early hours to toilet or not toileting at the regular time or perhaps just not looking their normal self, then it may mean that there is an underlying medical issue. Even if you cannot claim to be medically trained in any way, there are some things that should make you think 'is everything as it should be health-wise with my dog?'

For example, the onset of epilepsy might be flagged up if your dog has suddenly started to show signs of aggression towards family members, visitors or have 'blank' moments or shakes for no apparent reason. If your dog is usually 'buzzy' and is then rather quiet or vice versa, then take a trip to the vets. If it has grown up and just gradually become more of a hooligan as he matures, then it most probably is a purely behavioural issue. Dogs can't tell us if they don't feel well, but they are able to indicate that something is wrong.

The Ideal Recall

Before recalling your dog make sure you're worth coming back to. If you're angry or permanently grumpy, if your idea of getting your best friend to come back to you is to bellow like a Sergeant Major because you think it makes it sound like you're in charge, think again. Just as bad as the macho roar is the boring bleat, like a caricature of a Health and Safety Officer from Penge. If you're not worth coming back to then why should your dog bother? Motivate yourself, be welcoming, lighten your voice but most of all, get a pulse.

I will outline the full system in detail below which is for the baseball-cap-wearing dog who, when called, responds as though saying, "Talk to the paw." For other more amenable dogs you can use the appropriate level of discipline required for that individual. Most dogs will, as you implement the five components of PURE Dog Listening, return to you as soon as you call them. But there's always got to be one, hasn't there?...a complete and utter *Kevin* and it's sod's law that it's going to be your dog. Don't worry, by following the method shown below, which is known only to us and two Ecuadorian goat herders, there will be peace and love throughout the world and the sea will be full of fish again.

You will need a long line (not a flexi-lead) - those light nylon or webbing lines, just like a long traditional lead with a handle at one end and a clip at the other. They come in lengths from about 20 to 50 feet. My preference is the longer the better. You can buy these online if your pet shop doesn't stock them.

Ideally you will have two training venues. One very quiet place to teach the exercise and another - maybe a park - where the dog has the opportunity to be distracted by other dogs, joggers etc. but realises they still have to come back first time, every time.

Teaching the full method comes in three parts. You can do the first two at any time, but should only proceed to the last reinforcing lesson when the dog has pretty much given up leadership and is responding well in all other areas.

Part 1

Go to your quiet location and replace the normal lead with the long line. Let the dog bumble about doing their own thing. When the dog is not looking at you but engaged in some other interesting sight or smell then recall them. It is vital that you use a warm welcoming voice. Call the dog by name. When they look at you give really warm eye contact, arms open in a welcoming manner saying, "Good boy/girl, come." If the dog responds, keep the warm eye contact going as they come to you and on arrival give huge amounts of praise - they're the best thing since sliced bread. You then release again almost at once although keeping your dog still on the line.

Continue recalling with loads of praise as the reward. You can give the odd treat if you wish just to keep the dog guessing. No matter how many times you get a recall, eventually the time will come when you call him/her and the response will be "Whatever" and you'll be ignored. As soon as that happens, the warm eye contact goes, as does the happy encouraging voice. Turn your head away 45 degrees and pull the dog to you. Do not yank but just smoothly reel him in arm over arm as if you were pulling a boat in. When the dog is back with you just hold them silently at your side while you admire nature. No speech, no eye contact. This is the outdoor equivalent of isolating a dog in another room at home. You can hold them for two minutes if you're really miffed but generally hold just long enough to make the point.

When you release the dog after they've recalled well it is done in a happy way. In this instance you just step away from the dog and allow them to wander again. This is similar to releasing a dog from isolation in the home setting, just open the door and walk away. This allows the dog to rejoin the pack in a low key manner. Outside, the dog is going to consider: "That didn't go down too well. Let me think. I come back when called, I get loads of praise and maybe a treat. I get called and blank them, but I still have to go back, so I really have no choice. I might as well go back every time and get the positive welcome."

Once that is understood move on to:

Part 2

At the second venue repeat Part 1 with more activity. This section is exactly the same as part one except that the dog learns that whatever else that is going on: dogs, ball games, joggers etc., he/she should still return to you every time. When you have that sorted and you are happy that leadership has been relinquished or at the very least, the dog is responding really well to all the other signals, move on to:

Part 3

For this I advise my clients that if they have a video camera they should take it with them because their dog's facial expressions are likely to be amazing. Return to the first location, but before you do, visit your nearest supermarket! Go to the hot food counter and buy a whole hot chicken. These are what people buy when they arrive home late from work and don't have time or can't be bothered to cook. Once you have removed all the skin, fat and gristle there's not a huge amount of meat on them but for our purpose it doesn't matter. Take the bird home and strip it. Only discard the carcase, everything else - skin, fat, flesh and gristle - goes into a strong plastic bag which you take to the training venue.

Proceed as before, except that this time when the dog comes when called they not only get praise but also a small piece of the chicken. Of course it won't be hot now but it will be warm, tepid, slimy and clammy…like a politician's handshake. Repeat four or five times until you are confident of a solid recall. You can now release the dog. If you are still lacking in self confidence you can just drop the line rather than un-clip it. This gives you the opportunity to stand on it again to regain control if you need to. When the dog is released allow him/her to go a little further than they were able when on the line. Recall the dog in exactly the same way as you did when they were restricted by the line. As the dog approaches you in a perfect recall, get the remainder of the chicken - which will be 90% to 95% - and throw it on the ground in front of you. The dog will do a double take as if to say, "He's only gone and chucked a whole chicken on the ground, that's all! That can't be right." He will look at you in an enquiring way. You will say, "Good lad." He will say, "For me?" You'll say, "Yes." He'll say, "Woo-Hoo!!"…and will eat it up. Obviously you have to imagine the dialogue, but you can see the dog working it out as if the conversation was taking place. Once you reach this point the dog will always recall just in case you have another hot cooked chicken secreted about your person. He will just have to come back to check.

This scenario would, of course, have to be amended if dealing with a small dog such as a Chihuahua. Whatever you decide to use it must be a substantial reward for the dog rather than just a nice treat. They have to know something out of the ordinary has taken place. There has to be a Wow-Factor! You must not attempt part three too early because if the dog still thinks it is the leader then free chickens are their right.

The idea comes from a documentary film I watched about a wolf pack. They had young which were almost but not quite ready to join the rest of the pack on the hunt. The pack, while out hunting, were shot at and they lost the alpha female which of course caused uproar. The alpha male was grieving but almost at once a she-wolf approached him "Hello, big boy. I understand there's a vacancy." The male rejected her advances which continued over several days. Each rebuff caused her to bully the pups. The aggression got worse until she attacked the smallest of the she pups. The biggest of the dog pups put himself in between, to protect his sister and got bitten for his troubles. The next time the pack hunted the youngsters went along as well. They killed and as usual the pack backed off, to give the Alpha first go of the kill (Priority Feeding). He approached the carcase, stopped, looked around the pack and then went over to the dog pup who had protected his sister. He almost put his arm around him - he brought him forward and let the pup eat first. As the pup was eating Dad looked at the other pack members as if to say "That's my boy." It was a one off but the alpha wanted a way of rewarding behaviour that he was very happy with. In a much less dramatic way we are telling the dog that we are very happy with their behaviour and that good things happen to good dogs..."Stick with me kid and I'll take care of you."

It is long winded but it does work. As I said, for many dogs just the long line and praise is enough.

Take from it what you will and I hope you find it useful.

Recall With Two Dogs

If you call one dog and the other comes as well as, or instead of, the invited dog, disregard the interloper, maybe even hold him away by its collar if he insists on butting in and only interact with the dog that you've called. You are the leader and decide who may approach the throne. If you ignore such behaviour they will realise that they can present a united front against you. It is also important that dogs realise that they are individuals.

When dealing with negative behaviour that both are involved in always deal with the ringleader first.

Separation Anxiety

Why do dogs have separation anxiety? Well, the simple reason being that they feel responsible for you, that's all. Just imagine if your toddler got up and started to walk upstairs, what would your reaction be? You'd follow to make sure they were safe, because you are their protector. Now if you then go out of the house and inadvertently lock yourself out and you have left your young child in the house, what would you do? You'd most probably try and break in!!

So putting it from the dog's point of view, if they are separated from the one they feel responsible for, then that is exactly what they are doing when they rip up the kitchen when you leave and why they will follow you constantly around the house.

As your child grows up and becomes an adult...will you then follow them as they approach the stairs? No, you wouldn't because you know they can look after themselves. Unless you show your dog that you are quite capable of looking after yourself and him and you are not his toddler to be watched at every move, then he will continue to feel responsible for you.

You may have been advised to crate your dog: this will mean your kitchen won't be wrecked but the dog still has a big problem.

We can sort this problem out in a kind and stress-free way for both you and your dog, so read on...

<u>Take the sting out of leaving</u>

1) When you're sitting comfortably (wherever you are) in the home, make sure you can move around in your chair without him/her reacting.
2) Make sure you can stand up sit down.
3) Walk to the sitting-room door and back.
4) Rattle the door knob and sit down, each time making sure the dog settles on your return - you may have to use a 'Calm Hold' to make this happen.
5) Then go behind the door for two seconds and return, and sit...each time not looking at or acknowledging the dog's reaction. You are

showing your dog that you can come and go without it having to worry or react.

6) Increase the time outside the door by seconds at first.

7) As you increase your time away (very gradually), if you have the facilities then leave by one door and return by another.

If your dog gets up and has trouble settling between your movements then just bring the dog close to you and use a 'Calm Hold' until he relaxes and lays down. Then continue after a short time so he relaxes further. By doing this you are showing your dog that there really isn't an issue. You are completely relaxed and therefore so can he.

You will need a huge amount of patience and time in some cases, so stick with it and you and your dog will be rewarded.

If when you return from any of the exits the dog is overly distressed, it means you have been out too long. Go back to the period of time that the dog coped in your absence and move on from there. You will get to a stage when the dog does not react to your movement and stays relaxed wherever he may be. Do not get misled that your dog can only be relaxed in their bed. Remember though to use your doors so your dog doesn't have the opportunity to follow you everywhere. You will be showing him that you do not need a bodyguard - you can look after yourself.

The reason you exit so gradually is that the dog

doesn't have time to get too upset, and when you return your dog will settle quicker as it's adrenaline will not have shot up off the scale.

Do this 'Take the sting out of leaving' until you are so bored of it you could post a rotten egg through our letter boxes!...but your dog sleeps.

You are really showing the dog that it is off duty - you can go about your daily business without him having to follow all the time and he start to enjoy true relaxation, only having to get up when really necessary, like for a cuddle, a walk or a play, a potter to the water bowl or garden to lay in the sun.

If your mother or a friend was staying, you'd do the same for them - in a rather different way you'd tell them to relax, that they are on holiday and you are there to pamper them, and in this way stop them feeling they have to help all the time. I (Caroline) hate anyone in my kitchen and my worst nightmare is either my mother or mother-in-law fiddling around when I'm cooking. So relax they have to, talk to me by all means, but don't tell me how to cook or get in my way!

You can easily incorporate this method into daily life as with everything else. For instance, if you are in the sitting-room and wish to make a cuppa, then break it down into three or four steps. Go out of the room and shut the door and put the kettle on, then return, disregarding your dog's approaches. When settled, go out of the room again and get a cup from the cupboard, return as above and then go out and put a tea bag in the cup. Return, then go back out and at this stage you may have to boil the kettle again! All in a good cause though - dog training. A very long-winded way of making a simple cuppa but you do get one in the end. You have also taught your dog a valuable lesson - you don't need them with you all the time to survive.

How about the same process when you are doing the ironing, and ladies, this may be a way of getting your jobs done by other members of the family, as you will all have to do this in turn! You can tell Robin didn't write this bit, eh?! Mind you, he is pretty handy about the house, I'm told.

If there is more than one person in the household, when the family are all seated around the TV in the evening, then do take turns and practise 'taking the sting out of leaving' together. By doing this you are all showing him that you can take care of yourselves. If one member leaves the room and your dog is anxious and/or pacing, any member still in the room can gently go up to the dog and take him by the collar, then draw him close for a 'Calm Hold' without a word. You'll be showing him that you have no concerns about that person leaving and he will feel your calmness.

As calmness sets in you can extend this to leaving the house. From sitting reading the paper you can get up and walk out the front door. When you return very shortly after you walk in, just sit down, pick up the paper and carry on reading just as if you'd been to the bathroom. You can extend the time before returning, or leave by the front door and return via the back door. Several family members could leave at once and return at ten second intervals or you could even time it so that some come in the front at the same time as others arrive via the back. You are only limited in what you do by your imagination. As leader you can go where you like, whenever you like, for as long as you like.

The reason we do this in silence is that if we say anything, we fuel his fear or compound an issue. Put a dog right in silence so he begins to think of his own free will and modifies his own behaviour. We must always remember that dogs don't talk, they watch and learn, they learn by example. We also learn by example, we trust by example. Just because someone says that they are the best at their job, you won't believe them until they really prove it to you.

Mouthing

Mouthing is wholly unacceptable as a puppy or adult - dogs jaws are strong and there may be a time when they put too much pressure on and hurt. Especially important if you have or come into contact with children. Remember mouthing the wrong person could be construed as a bite and then you're in trouble. If a puppy or dog mouths or nibbles, then walk away from the moment and disregard the dog for five or ten minutes, then recall again to you and stroke calmly with little vocal stimulus (which might fire the dog up) and you're more likely to stop the unacceptable behaviour quicker. If you are over zealous in your stroking and/or over verbal then you will simply wind the dog up and the result will be mouthing, nipping or jumping up. If you have a 'buzzy' dog, you will have to learn to be calmer around it – it is very easy to over-excite a dog without meaning to.

Smiling Dogs

Some dogs do smile - they have learnt to mimic the human and the mimic gets a reaction, a positive reaction from humans, so well worth doing from a dog's point of view. People find the smile endearing, likening it to the human smile of welcome. The smiling dog has no fight on his mind, there is no growl or fearsome eyes or aggressive stance.

Also be aware, however, that in general when dogs show their teeth - their weapons - it's most definitely a warning. When I call a strange dog to me, I do make a point of not showing my teeth. I smile with closed lips and a kind voice. Then there is no doubt that I'm a friend.

Aggression

There are many different personalities out there in every living being, whether you are talking about humans, dogs, horses or sheep etc. - there are the shy ones, the full on 'don't mess with me' ones and the 'I'll go along with anything' ones.

The aggressive dogs that hit the headlines are generally the large fashionable dogs, often known as status dogs. However there are just as many, if not more, aggressive little dogs out there - they just don't hit the headlines because they don't kill or maim. They still have just as much intent though, ask any postman or delivery driver!

Aggressive...moi?!

When I am called out to any dog I ask the breed, not because I'm breedist!…just because I need to know what precautions I need to take: is it small and just going to scratch my ankle, or will I end up in hospital with an arm hanging off?

Within every breed there are different personalities and in every litter also…as with children, you get what you're given but you can nurture and bring them up positively - if bad behaviour is shown then you can help modify the behaviour so they can be accepted wherever they go.

Dogs will be aggressive if they are put in a position where they feel they ought or need to protect. There are some personalities that wouldn't dream of showing their teeth and would prefer to just run off, there are some that will bare their teeth and then run off…then there are the ones who really mean business!

Dogs will be fearful of potential threats…whether *we* think they are a threat or not. It is up to the owner to respond in the correct manner to show the dog that their fears are unfounded and there is no issue. If we shout at the dog to 'shut up' we are only fuelling the fire.

Who is there to decide what is a 'danger'…? If we get it wrong then it is the dog…in this case you have to trade places with your dog and show it that *you* will make the right decisions when appropriate, not him.

I hear some say, "But my dog growls at me, not

other people!" This is just your dog putting you in your place...the caring leader, just giving his subordinate a ticking off..."If you do that you'll get hurt" or "Don't sit there, that's the King's place" and "Who are you to tell me what to do?" or "Get away from my food." Attitude! It's just the same as you telling your child not to do something or "get up, that's my chair," but dogs can't talk - they only show their status. So we have to show them that we are the top guys and 'you can't push me around mate!' The way we do this is in a gentle and considerate way, with kindness and empathy. Don't get into a fight with your dog because you will come off far worse than he or she - you can't demand submission, you have to act like the adult and above all keep safe.

Don't try and make your dog submit by forcing it on its side and holding it down (you could well be setting yourself up for a disaster). Give it the right information so that it naturally submits to you, because of the way you are and not because you have resorted to force. Take a look at page 97 for the 'Three Levels of Discipline'.

Food Aggression

People have been taught to stop a dog being aggressive with food to keep taking the bowl away while it is feeding. Well, I (Caroline) can tell you most certainly that if you gave me a chocolate bar and then decided to take it from me half way through, you'd have a fight on your hands...you might even make me angry and aggressive!! You gave it to me and now you want it back?? Yeah right - you can't make your mind up?? Depending on your personality you may do one of two things:

1) Give it to me for a quiet life
or
2) Fight me for it

Don't set yourself up for a failure: if you give, then just do that – give. Don't go confusing signals. Don't tease a dog with anything and particularly not with food. You are messing with survival instincts if you do. Also, do read the section on Enhanced Priority Feeding again which will help reinforce some key points.

On Lead Aggression

So your dog may be great off lead running around the park, playing with other dogs and people. But… the big 'BUT'…when on lead some people find that their dog is aggressive to other dogs (and other things). From the dog's perspective, when it is off lead it is free to run away whenever it feels things are not quite right or feels threatened. If that dog is on the lead then they have lost the option of 'Flight' - they are tethered and cannot make the decision to flee…the only options left to them are 'Freeze' or 'Fight'. They can't get away so the only true option that is left is to get in there, show agression and prepare for 'Fight'. Some dogs are all mouth and no action, and may spend much of their time just barking ferociously. This is still a dog making decisions saying, "stay out of our space or else."

Even if he's always backed off, one day he may feel like he has no option but to bite.

If your dog trusts you to make the right decision, when he sees danger then he will be happy by your side for *you* to either take the 'Flight', 'Freeze' or 'Fight' option. We won't be doing any of the 'Fight' option (unless training a Police dog), but select the option that will make your dog feel safe in your hands and choose to follow your lead:

o If you take flight before he even reacts, you are simply changing the direction of your walk.

o If you take flight when he is thinking about being concerned, you're taking his mind off the object of focus and on to you and showing him that you're not in the least concerned.

o If he has reacted with barking and lunging and you then turn, you are showing him that there is no need for that - evasive action and keeping safe is better – and always praise and reward at heel...bish, bosh: sorted.

Dogs are reactive. We have the capacity to be proactive, dogs generally do not.

Walk away, your dog has to follow - he's on a lead - say nothing, don't tug and increase the pain, be that strong silent type that doesn't get into a fight. Praise your dog when he is back at heel, your dog will thank you for making a great decision. As we discussed when talking about the walk (Component

3) you can practise not getting into confrontation with the help of stooges. No dog truly wants to fight - give them the chance to walk away without losing face and they'll be happy.

Inter-Pack Aggression

We often get a call from an owner whose dogs are fighting between themselves. This generally happens when the owners enter the room and not when the dogs are left alone together. If this only happens when the owners are present, it is an indication of hierarchy 'discussions' and a debate about who's looking after the pack when they are all together. Both dogs think they are the one capable of the job and literally fight for it. Now, if the job of leader was taken by the human then these discussions would not be necessary.

Another situation when this may happen is if there is what we would refer to as 'a bully in the pack', and the attacks will seem unprovoked. It may be just a growl, a look, a nip or a full-on attack - intimidation is being used to keep all in their place. The aggression may be apparent at feeding time, or walking through narrow doorways, when one has possession of a toy, when non-household members enter the house or on a walk when they are both attached to a lead and something ahead is clearly a concern. Also, interestingly, sometimes one dog resting in bed or under a table will growl at another as it passes – saying, "My space, don't come close unless invited, I'm boss. Got It?"

Can you see a pattern here? The five components we talk about are very apparent: they are within times of danger, feeding, trophy possession, who goes through the door first and who is top dog when the pack rejoins.

Each time we are called to situations like these, we evaluate what all the dogs are doing and devise a plan of action that will either sort the issue out or put in place strategies to manage the situation. What we decide to do is directed by the personalities and the issues present.

Jumping Up

Why does your dog jump up at you or at visitors or on a walk at people you meet? Contrary to popular belief it is not because it is pleased to see everyone, let alone strangers. If you or your children were to do this then you would not be very well accepted into society. So why do we let dogs get away with it? While the common misconception is that your dog is so pleased to see people, I'm sure not everyone is pleased when their best suit has to visit the dry cleaners, not to mention those poor people who are afraid of dogs, who have to endure such boisterous physical contact with your four-legged friend.

With a puppy this is their natural behaviour when their mother returns, encouraging her to regurgitate her food by licking her mouth. Our heads are a lot higher than a canine mother's and therefore they jump higher, but if we misinterpret and thus encourage this behaviour they learn they can get attention and it then turns into demanding behaviour. This, as they grow up can indicate a dominance issue, so with an adolescent or adult dog you are really dealing with a dog in a panic and/or a dog taking control of a situation, checking out the opposition and entering your personal space. The dog has no self-control and is just calling the shots. It is not always a dog trying to get your attention, it is most often a dog having been put in a position of decision maker and trying to do just that, but it is out of its depth in our human world, a world it does not understand.

Who's in control when you re-enter the house or a room? Your dog is if it asks for attention and gets it.

If this is happening to you, whenever you see the behaviour, simply (without a word) push the dog off gently and say nothing, while not engaging in any eye contact. Repeat three times: if he does not get the message then isolate him without a word for ten seconds of quiet behind the nearest door. If you can't catch your dog, then *you* walk out of the room and re-enter when the dog is quiet and repeat if necessary. It is a battle of wits and determination - if you are determined, you will make it happen. If you say anything, he's got your attention whether it's in a positive or negative tone.

As PURE Dog Listeners we don't use any negative vocals - we teach by example and then praise and reward when the dogs have responded well. So if when you walk in a room and a dog disregards you while you hang your coat up and make a cup of tea, then you can then call the dog over for a cuddle. So the reward is given for not getting in your way when it's not convenient, and the message is clear that your dog will get called over quicker for a cuddle or a play as a result.

People often say that when they tell their dog to get 'down' it does, but they always have to say it. Wouldn't it be lovely if you didn't have to say that anymore and the dog respected your personal space without a word?

Pulling on lead

So off you go for your daily walk, your dog going over-the-top when the lead comes out and you have to rugby tackle it to get the thing on in the first place! You've started your walk off in the house with all guns blazing before you even venture out of the door. You're heading for failure, right from the word go.

Wild dogs do not naturally just go for a walk, this is a human thing. We must also understand that even though our dogs are not wild animals, they still have their natural instincts as do we when push comes to shove. Mainly, who is provider and protector and decision maker here? Are we safe and do we have food and access to water.

Your dog, pulling on the lead, is out there in front leading the way and keeping a look-out for food and danger. Panting and pulling. Now pulling does hurt, both you and your dog (probably not so much you, if your dog happens to be a Yorkshire terrier). It is also not a lot of fun for either of you. You need to be able to show your dog that it is you it needs to follow, to watch, and that being by your side is not only fun but a safe place to be. We teach heeling as a 'follow my leader game', slow but sure, starting at home in a calm environment where they are no distractions or concerns. You can both relax and have fun learning who follows who.

We do not advocate tugging to force your dog to be by your side: our aim is for your dog to want to be by your side, not because you may shout at it or add to his pain by tugging the lead, but because he sees it as a safe place and you as the decision maker and the leader of the walk.

This is another reason why on the lead an apparently relaxed dog will heel but, put a threat in its way and it will lunge and drag you down the road. A dog is by your side either because you have given it loads of food reward or you have deepened your voice and said, "No" and tugged it back in line. So your dog heels because it responds to food or tugging. The problem arises when there is a situation where the dog perceives something to be a threat. Then all that training goes out the window! What you have done is teach your dog to heel but for no meaty reason, apart from food or tugging and a grumpy voice. We want your dog to have a reason to walk next to you: it should be a place of safety in the knowledge that you will take the correct line of action when there is doubt. We teach you how to get your dog to elect to be by your side because it trusts you and understands you to be the unwavering decision maker, who makes good decisions for you and him.

Heel work should be fun and light-hearted, not a square bashing session. You've got to get your dog to follow you, have fun doing it and feel safe too. And what better way to do that than to play 'follow my leader' with praise and reward.

The problem occurs because when we go for a walk we go in a straight line and pay little attention to the dog. By heading off and keeping to a straight line the dog logs on to your direction and logs off of you. So keep changing direction, stop regularly, and always praise and reward when he gets it right. If he pulls in front, turn around and walk the other way saying nothing. When he is at your side praise and reward. Make it into a fun interaction and a game of 'follow my leader'.

This, like all the initial training, starts at home where there is little or no distraction and you can both become confident in each other. Then move to the outside world slowly but surely, keeping up the direction change. Whatever he pulls after, change your direction. He will then, as time goes by, be logged on to you and where you're going, if you are less predictable.

If you are not the spontaneous type you can make this easier by looking ahead when you go out. Decide that when you reach that parked red car you will cross to the opposite footpath and when you get to the house with the green gate you'll cross back again. When you reach the pillar box maybe you could do an about turn for ten yards before retracing your steps. By doing this your dog will learn that you change direction 'because you can' and not for a particular reason. This is very useful if you suddenly encounter a threat while on your walk, when you cross the road your dog will not wonder why, and pulse rates and stress levels stay low.

When you practise heel work it is generally done in a fairly artificial environment like the village hall and this can become the only venue when the dog does walk to heel, and often reverts to previous poor behaviour when leaving the hall. We can also come across situations where we cannot get the heel as there is a distraction the dog is more aware of than being by your side, whether that be danger, scent sniffing or other four legged animals such as rabbits (food on legs to a dog). Teach him as above and you'll keep him thinking about you and not to concern himself with everything else.

Excessive Barking

Post flying through the door. What is it? Is it going to kill us? I'll bark, that'll show him! 'I'll kill the paper', thinks the dog! Postmen and paperboys are always fair game for dogs. They come at more or less the same time everyday, they rattle the letterbox and poke stuff through, that's their routine. The dog develops a routine as well. At 07.05a.m. the paperboy arrives and the dog barks,

"Clear off!" And he does. Dog thinks 'That told him, he won't try that again'. At 08.30a.m. the postman arrives and we have a repeat performance, where the dog successfully repels the perceived attack. Of course neither paperboy nor postman learn their lesson and tomorrow morning they'll be back again and up to their old tricks, which really provokes the dog and raises their stress levels. Won't these humans ever learn?

It is as straightforward as that. Remember dogs do not understand our world and all we have - there is no reason why they should. We have to show them that post really isn't a problem for us and the postman or visitor hasn't come here to kill either. If we make nothing of something it will become nothing, as if we make something of nothing it will become something.

If we shout and scream, "stop it" the dog just thinks you're joining in too and rips it up more or barks more and you end up with a hoarse voice and red in the face!

Let's approach it from a different angle and show the dog our gratitude for warning us of pending danger, then *we* take charge of the situation in a cool, calm and collected manner so that the dog sees that we are dealing with what he perceived as danger and placing him in the back seat. 'What a relief' the dog thinks!

Remember the dog is very much in touch with its basic instincts: 'are we safe?' and 'is there food to survive?' These instincts are geared to promoting survival and keeping the pack safe…all life and death stuff. We don't want to sound too dramatic, but when we first domesticated the wolf all those thousands of years ago we lived as wild animals do now. Our larder was our hunting ground and our base was our safe place, woe betide another tribe encroaching on that. Can't really imagine there was much entertaining in those times or having your neighbours around for dinner either!! We had to protect our own and sharing a hard-earned feast with others when you didn't know when you'd have another successful hunt would most certainly not be in the equation. You and yours had to survive. If a neighbouring tribe entered your area you would fight tooth and nail to preserve your life support, your hunting ground and your property.

So for your dog to bark at the door is a good thing, a warning that there's something about. However, to continue to bark and bark is not only irritating to the next door neighbours and challenging for you, it is a dog in a huge panic, not knowing what to do and trying its hardest to ward off danger. Even if you can't see or hear anything that started it off, remember that your dog's sense of smell and hearing are far far greater than ours. Be the adult, take over and show him that all is fine and you can cope and he can chill out.

So, as previously mentioned when 'danger' presents itself, thank the dog for the warning and reward with a kind gesture - if he continues barking reassure him by looking out the window towards the danger and if he still continues barking take your dog by the collar and isolate him in the downstairs loo (if you have one and he fits in comfortably, otherwise choose another room away from the front door, preferably not the room he sleeps in). When he is quiet let him out, if he barks, repeat the isolation again for five seconds of quiet and repeat by increasing the time-out until he comes out and remains quiet. His reward is that he rejoins the pack and stays with the pack when quiet. You have shown him that you will decided whether there is danger or not and demonstrated that he should accept that all is fine.

Attention Barking

If you can, ignore it. If it is too much and you have neighbours banging on the walls, then I suggest you walk out of the room and when the dog is quiet, return. Say nothing to the dog and repeat as necessary. When the dog gives up and disregards you in the room then recall him for a cuddle and reward. Do remember with all these things you will have to show your dog 'as many times as it takes' to get it right. He may well try again the next evening and the next, but until you get your way do not give in. If you give in then he has won and he has your attention on his terms.

If you give your dog a chew to entertain itself at this stage then all you are doing is re-enforcing the behaviour. He's got your attention and every time he barks at you, you respond with food - he's got you wrapped around his paw! He's trained you to respond to his demands.

Car Trouble

Many dogs have trouble travelling in cars ranging from mild restlessness through anxiety to full blown hysteria. By using the techniques in this book you will be able to resolve these issues. Even in extreme cases you can overcome your dog's negative perception of travelling in a vehicle. The following should give you food for thought.

We have a group of friends and colleagues in the Southern Hemisphere doing similar work to us. In 2008 during the horrendous Victoria bush fires which left humans and animals dead or injured and homes and environments destroyed, many groups (including Dog Listeners) got heavily involved in rescue work with the 'Fire Dogs' as they became known. They'd lost their homes and maybe their families, some had a range of burns or other injuries, and all were traumatised. Even if the whole family had survived they had nowhere to live let alone look after their dogs. They travelled countless miles to collect dogs and take them to a place of safety where they could be worked with to de-traumatise them, keep them safe and in the happiest of cases reunite them with their original families.

Of course, in such rescue cases, one of the first things that had to be done was to get the dog into a vehicle - easier said than done. We are talking terrified and maybe aggressive (through fear) animals here. To simplify things one of the Dog Listeners, Lynne Fitzsimmons, wrote a simple step-by-step guide for use in these situations which, with her kind permission, we reproduce here:

o Lead-walk your dog to the car, making a point of changing direction a few times before you even go near the car and put the focus back on you - this reminds the dog who is making the decisions and in this instance, getting close to and into the car.

o It also makes a huge difference if you take a few minutes to bring the dog's adrenaline down before it gets into the car.

o Be careful not to fall into the trap of trying to pacify a dog with words, no matter how soothing. So avoid patting, stroking or even looking at them.

o Eye contact from a dog you don't know may be perceived as confrontational or even tip a very stressed dog over the edge. As we've said before, eye contact is the beginning of communication and if a dog is concerned then the eye contact from you is going to confirm his thoughts, no matter what comes out of your mouth.

o If you're transporting a dog you don't know, give him as much personal space as possible.

o If it is your own dog who has car trouble, then using the 'Calm Hold' for a short period in the back of the car is maybe all it needs.

o Having the dog on a long lead no matter where or how far back in the car it is, enables you to put the slightest tension on it at certain times and this can stop the dog from over-reacting.

o Just having the lead on your shoulder seems to calm some dogs as they can feel your energy down the lead. The lead also allows you to apply a gentle calming pressure if necessary.

o Stopping ten minutes down the road, pulling over and opening up the back and just sitting next to the dog and letting them have a drink if need be can help reduce stress levels. This can help the dog that got in and started the 'stressed panting thing' quite quickly, as it can help break their stressful mind-set and then continue without panting.

o Dogs in covered crates with the crate safely anchored also helps reduce stress when travelling with a dog in the car - they have no visuals and can hide.

o Maybe try to use newspaper to block out the side windows so you still have rear vision but the dogs won't get that 'flashing past' effect as you drive along.

o Lots of dogs do much better if they are low to the bottom of the car in a foot-well.

o Tethering dogs so they can't run or spin also helps.

o Changing the location of the dogs in the car also can make a huge difference.

We hope something in here gives you an idea you can try. As you can see the story is always the same, whatever problem you're dealng with. Keep it calm and don't put stress on the dog - they've had enough of that already. Just be that rock that silently says everything is in hand, there's no danger anymore.

Running Off and Chasing Animals

As far as your dog is aware when out and about walking with you, you are out on the hunt. But you have done the weekly shopping and you don't need any extra!...but your dog doesn't know that.

Your dog is most probably having a great time but he is out there in front taking the lead and you are dutifully following him. Calling and calling your dog, who does not respond, is only reassuring him that you are there and when he wants to he can find you easily.

A lot of dogs will look back to see you are there and then carry on in the direction they were going, they are happy in the knowledge that you are trying to keep up with them on their hunt, regardless of the fact that you are going blue in the face shouting for them to return!

We need your dog to be tuned into you, so he follows you on your walk and not the other way around. If you don't feel like a rabbit or chicken chasing session then the hunt should be off in his eyes and head. Leader says, "No!" and then carry on for a lovely relaxed walk. Rather than your dog on his walk and you on yours, wouldn't it be so lovely to be together and enjoy the company of each other?

Make sure that your lead work and recall is perfect at home and wherever you walk your dog before you try off lead where there are distractions. Build it up gradually, and don't expect his recall to be perfect in the middle of the park or rabbit warren even if it is perfect at home.

Marking and Defecating in the house

Puppies soil in the house when we first get them, but within a few weeks we hope to have taught it the correct place to go to the toilet – outside in an appropriate place. Both dogs and puppies relieve themselves at fairly predictable times: after sleeping, after eating, at the beginning of a walk for example. They will also give you a signal if you are alert enough to spot it. The easiest dogs are the ones who go to the back door and give a gentle bark or maybe a scratch. The quieter dog might just sit by the door hoping that a human will read the signal. Younger or less confident dogs might appear restless and pace in the house. If they start to circle then your dog is running out of options and can't wait. With young puppies, as with young children, the connection to the brain that alerts them to the need for a toilet break is not made. Even when the connection is made, puppies - like children - can become so engrossed in the game they're playing that accidents happen. The best way to tackle this is as always to take the stress away from both you and the dog. Maximise your chances of success and in so doing make it possible to legitimately praise your puppy.

Each time the puppy has eaten do take it outside. When it performs one or the other then reward with food and praise. If a puppy has woken up from sleep then take it outside to relieve itself and food reward when it does what is required. If he has an accident in the house, say nothing and just clean it up. Puppy will think 'I get nothing in the house for my present but get praise and reward outside' and he will soon learn. If you tell him off when he's done it inside he may wet himself out of fear or think 'Hey, that's another way to get attention'.

You wouldn't punish a young child for having an accident. They didn't mean to - it's uncomfortable and maybe embarrassing for them, so why compound their misery? They grow up, they get bladder control and they're fine. It's all a game of patience and understanding.

Now with older dogs this is an anxiety problem (unless it has a bladder infection or bowel problem). Some dogs hate going outside, some will even (having gone for a long walk) wait until they get home and inside until they perform. If a dog has to have its wits about him while you're out and about, ready to spring into action at any moment, he can't relax and do his business and you wouldn't be able to either. If you were to take the luxury of relieving yourself, you would be immobilised and therefore vulnerable. Also, if you're tense then you can't relax enough to perform anyway. Dogs are individuals and some, if really anxious, will have loose motions when out on a walk where this may not be the case in the back garden.

Some dogs urinate when visitors arrive - this is a sign of being nervous/anxious. If only your visitors would leave the dog alone and not invade its space then it wouldn't happen. Some dogs do this with their owners, often if the owners go into a dog's space rather than call the dog to them.

Other dogs may do this when you're out - a sign either of separation anxiety or that you've left them too long. Take a look at the earlier section on Separation Anxiety.

<u>Excessive Marking on the walk</u>

Dogs mark to tell other dogs that they've been there and that it's their territory, even though we know it is not really their or our territory: it is a shared territory. Your dog, by leaving messages like this constantly on a walk, is a dog with a job and not truly relaxing into the fun factor and enjoyment of the exercise. He's too busy letting everyone else know he's about. The higher the scent mark the greater chance it has to catch the wind and travel further. We've seen dogs that will almost do a handstand to get their mark higher up a lamp post to ensure that as many get the message as possible.

I suppose you could liken this to an advertising leaflet drop...doing a job to advertise yourself or a company as the biggest and best in your field. The point is that you are working, and not going out for pleasure.

Show your dog this is not a job that needs to be done - if he pulls towards a marking post, wall, gate or other suitable point, do not let him dictate your movement. For a start off he's controlling your movement and therefore in charge and secondly he's doing the unnecessary work of leaving messages, advertising his presence - the big boy on the block.

All you have to do is simply and silently guide him away by changing direction. When he is at your side praise him, maybe offer a food reward initially and carry on your way. You've made nothing of what he was intending to do and shown him it is not necessary. You're taking him for a walk and not a boundary marking session.

Bitches will sometimes also mark like this - the solution is the same.

Attacking the Vacuum Cleaner and/or Broom

Ensure your dog is relaxed before you start anything and you will get a far better response. Pick the broom up (don't look at the dog) and turn it the wrong way up as if it's a walking stick! If the dog reacts then stop and put it down and do something else. Try again. It may be worth having the dog on a short lead and doing some silent lead work and then pick the broom up, hold the dog at arm's length on the left and the broom on the right and sweep away from him. If the dog gets upset then stop and try again when the dog is calmer.

Do likewise with the vacuum cleaner. Why not just have it out in the room as a new ornament, so the dog gets used to it just sitting there. Walk past it every now and again and touch it. In a day or so walk past and turn it on and off and walk away, making absolutely nothing of it. The slower you do all this the better. When you do vacuum then start off in the furthest part of the house away from the dog. If you live in a very small space and this is not practical or possible, then <u>never push the appliance towards the dog</u>, focusing on having your side view facing the dog.

It may be better, particularly if your dog gets very upset by these things, to be separated by a baby gate initially and when the dog reacts then simply stop and shut the solid door until he is calm, then begin again.

With a lot of these problems it is a great idea to start sorting these extra issues out when you have had a week or two of getting to grips with the basics of PDL i.e. the main five. This gives your dog time to understand where you are coming from and build trust in you and your decisions.

Do make sure there is an escape route for the dog, so if it simply wishes to take itself off to another room while you're doing the housework, then it can. There should be no pressure on the dog to watch and learn - you're never going to expect him to do the housework!

Do remember if your dog is very upset and aggressive, get a PURE Dog Listener in to advise and help.

A Dog that Won't Play Ball

If you can't relax then usually you won't be able to play and enjoy yourself. Dogs are great play animals - they learn through play - but if you're the one with responsibilities of survival then that will be last on your agenda.

So take the responsibility away and then your dog will relax and you'll be able to teach him that play is fun wherever you are. Some dogs will play in the garden but not out and about: they are relaxed in the garden or house and struggle out of their safe zone. Take responsibility away from them and find the lovely, happy dog in there you never knew existed.

Tail Chasing

This is another behaviour a dog does when he is in a pickle and doesn't know what to do. He may have done it as a pup and everyone roared with laughter: he got a reaction and a positive one at that, and is just repeating the behaviour.

155

In many instances it becomes an obsessive behaviour and is simply put right by taking the dog by the collar and holding him until he relaxes. You then step away and repeat the procedure as necessary, with no eye contact and no vocals. Persevere - you may not solve this overnight but you'll be pleasantly surprised how quickly you'll see results.

Obsessive Light and Shadow Chasing

As with any obsession, do not compound the issue by laughing and engaging your dog: this is how it all started in the first place. Watches reflecting on walls, sunlight on the kitchen cabinets can prove all too interesting. If you make something of it it will become something to the dog. They don't understand what it is and just because you've made something of it in the past, he thinks that it *is* of interest or maybe an issue that needs his attention. Some may just try to catch it, some are rather more upset about it and will bark at it, but if it is a problem then it needs to be sorted out as soon as possible.

To stop this behaviour, simply guide the dog away from it without a word, maybe even take it into another room to take the attention away. If necessary do this a few times and either distract by changing room and doing something else or if he is really fired up then place him in a 'Calm Hold'. If he goes back for a fourth time, call him and maybe give him a toy to play with or place him in a 'Calm Hold' to rest.

Digging up the Garden

We've already mentioned how strange it is that we humans will allow some species their natural behaviour but not others. People who have rabbits and chickens don't give it another thought when they dig holes because that's what they do, and we can often ignore a cat who prepares a hole to defecate in. A dog, well, that's another matter. The fact is that it's just being a dog, as the cat, chicken and rabbit are just being themselves too. We never make a big deal of it with the other animals but we do with the dog as the hole is probably bigger. The other reason of course is that we expect the dog to abide by our human rules and mind-read, and we do so love telling our dogs what to do. Here's a thought to hang onto: instead of talking at your dog...try listening - Dog Listening. Keep it PURE and you'll be amazed what you'll hear. Take Ronan Keating's advice: "You say it best when you say nothing at all."

Your plants and plant pots may well be your pride and joy come the spring and summer. Then you get a dog who has designs on being the next Alan Titchmarsh in the family. His fingers are not green and the only redesigning he has done has turned the garden into your worst nightmare! Do not make a big drama out of it, because if you do he will have got your attention and will very likely do it bigger and better next time. However mad you feel, just take your dog by the collar and lead him away, 'Calm Hold' in silence for a minute, then clear up the mess. If your dog decides that he is going to turn this into a game of chase then back off and begin clearing up the pots (whether inside your house or outside) completely blanking him. Next time he is in the garden make sure you have a long line attached to his collar so you can take hold of it. If he makes a beeline for your begonias, reel him in and hold him for a minute or two in silence. Then release. Step away and when he is busy pottering or looking to go back to your plants then recall him to you and reward. Show him he is getting nothing for the destruction and everything for the good stuff. Do not leave your dog unattended in the garden if he has a long line on or indeed if he has a tendency to do the gardening. A time will come when you can trust him to behave.

With a young puppy who hasn't got into the pattern of obsessive digging yet, you could just do a simple recall and take him off to do something else. Either way he has not got any attention for what he has just been doing.

Dogs and Cuddles

Not all dogs like cuddles and strokes especially from strangers.

As mentioned already, we all love a good massage but we're certainly not going to get a complete stranger to do it!!

Dogs have their own personalities, likes and dislikes. Just because it's a dog and has fur doesn't mean it likes any Tom, Dick or Harry in close proximity!

Fussy Eaters

There is no such thing as a fussy eater. Dogs are opportunists and hunters. There are dogs that will manipulate you into feeding it when and what it wants - one week it will eat the supermarket special and stops the next week, so you try Jimmy's Own: he eats that for a week and then stops and looks lovingly at your steak and chips...he gets some and then you're on that slippery slope. You've made a rod for your own back and he's got you where he wants you: trained. I had a client who would drive to the very expensive delicatessen in the village every morning and buy a selection of cold meats for his dog to make his daily choice. He was very picky and what wasn't eaten today was thrown away because neither husband or wife liked cold meat. The following day the process was repeated. Within a week of the consultation the dog was eating what he was given and the wine list was a thing of the past. He was a lot happier in himself, looked healthier and life was a lot more pleasant for my clients when they cleared the garden. When a dog hunts in the wild his preferred prey is not chorizo, salami or black pudding!

Some dogs can't eat in the morning as they are so anxious about what is to confront them during the day.

Then, with some dogs, there are times that they lose their appetite every now and again due to something that has happened or changed within the dynamics of their human family/pack. Whatever the reason, this behavioural problem is very straightforward to correct.

If you're relaxed you can eat, and if you're not trying to prove a point and take control you can eat. There are five main times during a dog's day that tells it whether it is the main decision maker or not. One of these is who controls feeding times.

Frightened of Noise

Whether your dog is bothered by Bonfire night depends to some extent on his personality but mostly on your leadership, so what you do when your dog freaks out on November 5th is more important than what the dog does.

When we are scared we often feel better if someone puts a reassuring arm around our shoulders or offers a few soothing words. But dogs are not humans and to offer your dog a cuddle and to talk reassuringly to it when it is in an anxious state will make the situation worse: you are giving him attention for this behaviour and therefore re-enforcing the fear.

What a dog really needs from you at this time is good leadership which means convincing him that you are in charge and that there is absolutely nothing to worry about.

The key thing to remember is not to engage with your dog when it is stressed. This may be initially very difficult for many dog owners but it becomes second nature with a little practice. If the dog comes to you for attention or runs into a corner shaking, don't react. If necessary, just hold the dog still in a 'Calm Hold'. Take hold of his collar and draw him close to you, gently placing the palm of your hand over his shoulders, making gentle contact and wait for him to relax, not stroking him or engaging him in anyway - your dog will come to understand that you are calm. If you're not worried then he needn't be either. If you've ever been with someone who has just lost a loved one or had some other traumatic event, just placing your hand on theirs and saying nothing is the best thing you can do. You are saying silently that you are there.

Maybe your dog's fear of fireworks is just a symptom of something else. He possibly believes he is responsible for your safety, so try not to fuel this belief.

Dogs and Cats

If these are to get on well together at home then we need to think about some key points. For example, wherever possible provide a 'bolt hole' for the cat. It can be upstairs or in a particular room which is a no-go area for the dog. The 'off limits' status of this area can be reinforced by the use of a baby gate if required. Feed the cat in their safe area to relieve stress - a dog will always go for the cat's food because it's often left down longer than their food. They can, by eating it, enhance their status. Don't give them the chance.

To teach the animals to at least co-exist calmly,

implement the following strategy. You will need two people. Your assistant should wait outside or in another room with your dog.

o Have your cat sit with you at your side or on your lap. Hold the cat gently but firmly.

o Your assistant does a short period of 'Follow my Leader' by using the technique of random changes in both pace and direction, interspersed with unsignalled halts, outside the room. This is to really focus the dog and remind it to pay attention to the humans and not to anything else.

o Your assistant should enter the room with the dog on a lead. If the dog as much as looks at the cat, then immediately isolate.

o Repeat until the dog comes into room and lays down (still on lead) ignoring the cat. Then allow the cat to move.

o If the dog reacts to the cat's movement then isolate until the lesson is learned.

o As with all these techniques, don't rush. It takes as long as it takes. Keep calm and act like a leader making the point that you will not accept bad behaviour from subordinate animals. As the Alpha *you* decide who can be a pack member, not a dog or cat with 'issues'. Remember that although you can teach a dog that any cat that you bring into your home is a member of your pack, most dogs will still consider strange cats as fair game, at least for a while.

CHAPTER 8

Embarrassing problems

Bum Scooting (Bum Dragging)

We've all seen dogs do this, dragging their backsides across the floor as if taking part in the Winter Olympics only to find out that someone's stolen their toboggan. This is a common problem with an easy solution. Your dog probably has impacted anal glands and they need emptying. A quick trip to a vet will soon sort it out. You could even do it yourself at home, if you are adventurous and there happens to be nothing on television. I'd hazard a guess that if you try it once then the next time the procedure is needed you'll be down the vets as quickly as you can. Does it smell? Yes. Perhaps I should clarify that by saying, "Yes, disgustingly so." Does the dog mind? Once the glands are emptied the dog feels great relief but the process can annoy or cause them discomfort. It's hardly dignified - would you stand calmly discussing the weather while your back passage and vicinity was being squeezed and probed?

This could also be an indication that your dog has worms of some variety, so do ensure that he is regularly treated.

Coprophagia (Poo Eating)

Coprophagia is a very complex issue which can be fear based either to hide the fact that they've defecated from humans because they have been reprimanded for it in the past or it could be an attempt to hide their presence from other dogs. If a dog is eating its own waste, it is said that adding certain items to the food such as pineapple or courgettes makes the faeces unpalatable…like they were tasty before? It should go without saying that you add the pineapple or other chosen extra to the dog's food prior to feeding. It has been known for some owners who have been advised to try this method, rather than add to the food, they have kept their dog under observation and then as soon as they have defecated, have rushed out and placed a piece of pineapple on top of the still steaming mound like a cherry on top of a trifle. This variation on a theme is very colourful but generally does not work!

A cherry on top of a trifle or…?!

It could be too that the dog is not getting all they need from their present food, particularly if at a stage of rapid growth. As a guide to how a dog is managing with their food ask yourself, "Do they look healthy? Are they growing at the correct rate? Are their faeces firm and not foul smelling?" If you decide to change their food, do it gradually so that they don't get 'food A' one day and 'food B' the next. Before going to the hassle of a complete diet change try adding a pot of natural yogurt to their food to improve the digestion and absorption of all the nutrients from the food.

Mounting

When your dog decides to display mounting – more commonly called 'humping' – behaviour, it throws us humans into a state of embarrassment and confusion. "Why does he do that?" we ask. The answer is simple...because he's a dog and that is what dogs do. They don't have our sensibilities. They exhibit behaviour, any behaviour, because that seems to be the right thing to do at that time. Both dogs and bitches will mount, it matters not whether they are entire or neutered. They'll do it to other dogs of the same or opposite sex. They'll do it to their beds, cuddly toys or your favourite cushions and of course, worst of all, to humans. Most dog owners who are subjected to these displays by their dogs tell us that it occurs far more frequently when they have guests, particularly when they're trying to make a good impression. The vicar comes to tea or the boss comes to dinner and there is a possible promotion in the offing when, game on, the dog starts performing. We don't know how to deal with it so we often make a joke of it or get angry and shout at the dog. We can get embarrassed and pretend it's not happening. Sometimes the recipient of the dog's attentions even tries to casually walk away. Not so fast! The dog remains clamped to the leg as it is dragged across the room in a caricature of a Torvill and Dean Ice dance routine or an actor from the local Am Dram playing Richard the Third.

More tea, vicar…?!

It's almost as if the dog was doing this to show the owner up. They wouldn't do that, would they? Or would they…? Let's talk about sex and our perceptions and consider the canine perceptions here too. We humans are one of a very small number of species that engage in recreational sex. The majority of the animal kingdom, including canines, only has sex to procreate. In the wild, where pack behaviour can be more easily observed and understood, without all the interference of 'civilisation', it soon becomes clear that to a pack

166

animal the only thing that matters is that the pack survives. Everything else is subordinate to that goal. For that reason as explained elsewhere in this book the pack must have a leader...ideally an Alpha male and Alpha female who get the job by virtue of being the best, the fittest and most intelligent. Because of that they are usually (but not always) the only members of the pack to breed. If they are the best, then their offspring will be of a high quality and therefore maximize the continuing survival of the pack. If the lower ranking members breed the quality of pup goes down as does the survival probability of the pack. Think of the difference of a puppy from a reputable breeder and one from a puppy farm. The latter is most likely to be inferior in every way - health, build, intelligence and almost certainly lifespan.

So why is the dog causing such upset among the humans witnessing his amorous approaches to the vicar? He's almost certainly already gone through his repertoire of attention seeking behaviours and now needs to up the ante. What he or she is saying to their audience is, "Hey everybody! Look over here! I appear to be having sex with this person's leg. As only Alphas breed (and I'm busy impregnating the vicar) then that makes me the leader. You should therefore not be talking to my 'owner' but to me."

Once again it's just a matter of seeing what the dog sees in every situation and then we can resolve it.

Simply hold your dog away by the collar and wait for it to settle, repeat as necessary. Again, do not engage in any eye contact or talking as this is perceived as encouragement and reward.

The following is a light-hearted effort to get inside my dogs' heads – to explore why they dug ankle-breaking holes all over the lawn... Why, when they found a dead creature did they feel the need to either:

a. Eat it (then throw up)

b. Roll in it (then I'd throw up)

c. Present it to me (then I'd throw up)

...sounds like fun to me!

OH RATS!

I now know that they dig holes
a. because they can smell a burrowing creature
and they want to eat it
b. because they like it

They eat dead and smelly creatures
a. because it's food, and they are opportunists
b. because they like it

They roll in dead creatures
a. because they want the rest of the pack to share
the pleasure - and tell them where they can find the
source of the lovely smell - and eat it
b. because they like it

They bring me dead creatures
a. it is food, and as leaders
they are providing for me
b. they like to see me suffer.

By Leslie Harris

CHAPTER 9

Rescue dogs

Some dogs have been mistreated or are just plain confused. Some have had many homes, some maybe only one. In all cases they have been placed in a refuge for a variety of reasons. Many of these dogs were bought as fluffy little bundles of fun at about eight weeks of age. As a dog matures, it begins to need more food, more exercise and more of the owner's time. It also may have presented with behavioural problems that are unacceptable to their owners who find certain issues unworkable.

Re-homing these vulnerable dogs is not easy, as people often perceive older dogs to be untrainable but this is not the case. Using the communication skills of a PURE Dog Listener you can 'teach an old dog new tricks'. So bear in mind, if you do take on a rescue dog, it is going to need more time to gain that trust. Don't focus on its past, but make allowances for nervousness by being compassionate, calm and patient.

All dogs deserve to be understood. Whenever we are called to see such a dog with behavioural problems, a line is drawn on that day - what is past is past (we will never know what some rescue dogs have been through) and we focus on the future. We work with you to help you show your new friend that he is safe and secure in his new home. A feeling that all canines deserve, and which we should provide.

CHAPTER 10

Angry dogs

When Dogs Get Angry, Frightened or Annoyed,
They Don't Call Their Lawyer...They Bite.
That's What They Do.

50% Of All Dogs Will Have An Aggressive Encounter
With A Human In Their Lifetime!

A Dog Bite Can Cause Injuries: From Bruising To
Lacerations, Scarring And In Serious Cases Broken
Bones And Even Fatalities.

Don't Be Lulled Into A False Sense Of Security:
Remember, Any Dog – Whatever Their Size Or
Breed, **Can Turn From...**

**To
This**

➡

In a **Split Second...**

Why does my dog do that? Because…it's A DOG!

How can I avoid being bitten by a dog?

When you enter a dog's territory you may be perceived as a threat. Of course most dogs are perfectly friendly and the only danger you will face is being coated in hair and saliva. But if the dog is unsure of you and your intentions he will have three methods of dealing with the threat you pose:

Flight: If a dog can get away even to the bottom of the garden or into another room he will be happy. Under no circumstances approach him or attempt to placate him. If you restrict his ability to flee he will resort to the third option.

Freeze: If a dog doesn't want to interact - either fearful or shy - it may choose to stay very still. Usually if you ignore him he will be happy to return the favour.

Fight: A dog will react in this way if the first two methods have failed or he is a trained guard dog or he is a naturally aggressive Alpha, or (most probably) if you have given him the wrong signals.

What to do

If you need to visit an address where you have reason to believe a dog is running free, assess the situation before you enter. If you are worried, stay on the public side of the door/gate. Make contact with the occupants by calling out or by using your mobile phone. Ask them to either secure the dog or come out and deal with you at the gate.

If you do enter the property and are then approached by a dog, stand still, arms by your sides, not speaking and using no eye contact. Once you have been checked out and feel it's safe to move, do, but do it smoothly and calmly. Walk tall: you are an Alpha.

If once inside you are unhappy about the situation back slowly away still sticking rigidly to the 'no eye contact' and 'no speech' rule.

Remember, it takes no more time to think than it does to panic.

Ideally the owner should already have or be able to take control of the dog but not everyone realises that the world may not be in love with their dog. They are also blissfully unaware of the potential results if their dog becomes aggressive. "It's alright. He's only playing." Oh, so that's alright then. Even after their dog has bitten, some owners remain unperturbed. Their two favourite phrases are: "It's only a nip." or "It's your fault. You must have upset him." As you can see you cannot always rely on the owner to do the right thing so you need to look to your own safety in such cases.

If it becomes probable that you are about to be bitten try to give the dog a target - they will generally bite anything thrust at them so, a clipboard, briefcase or anything the dog can target rather than you is good. If they can pull it off of you then that item becomes a trophy and they will often run around with their prize allowing you to make your exit.

If the worst happens, try to keep on your feet. If knocked to the ground, curl into a ball with your hands over your ears and remain motionless. Try not to scream or roll around.

What not to do

Do **NOT**:
- o Shout at a dog
- o Show any aggression
- o Scream and/or run
- o Walk between owner and dog
- o Invade the dog's personal space
- o Go near a bitch with a litter

And most importantly, **NEVER** ignore any signals that the dog is giving you. Most dogs don't want to bite you, but if they feel they have to then they will mean it.

Dogs are not Walt Disney characters. A dog only knows how to be a dog. If we understand that and respect the dog we will usually have a safe resolution.

Status Dogs

This is a problem that has been steadily growing over the last few years and regrettably shows no signs of improvement.

What is a 'Status Dog'? It is any dog that the owner has to supplement their manhood, to look macho, to demand 'respect' and gain 'street cred', to use as a weapon against humans or to use in dog fighting or maybe they just need a dog to guard their drugs, money, weapons or maybe all three.

We all know the dogs, and certainly the owners that we're talking about here. The sad fact is that many of these status dogs would rather be that Labrador on the common or a lap dog in Rose Cottage, but they are not given the choice. The vast majority of these breeds are perfectly normal dogs that get tainted, often guilty by association. This can be a major problem for the responsible dog owner.

Status dogs come in and go out of fashion and to get 'respect' - not earn it you understand but 'get it' - these individuals feel they must always have the latest landshark.

Perhaps the first Status dog of the second half of the 20th Century was the German Shepherd or Alsatian. They are, contrary to some people's belief, the same breed, in fact there is no such breed as Alsatian. That is a name that was given to the breed when they arrived in the UK at the end of the First World War when anything with German connections was viewed with distrust.

The German Shepherd became more common in the UK after the Second World War when they were seen as Police dogs. A good looking dog that can bite was like a magnet to a certain type of inadequate and so demand grew. There were both quality breeders producing good fit animals for the discerning owner who loved the breed, and 'puppy farmers' who would mass breed with substandard stock in filthy conditions. The good breeder would, and still does, interview all potential buyers of their pups. All the puppy farmer was interested in was, and still is, whether the customer had the cash (and it's almost always cash - we wouldn't want to leave a paper trail and get involved in boring stuff like taxes, would we?)

The German Shepherd went out of fashion and was replaced at varying times by the Doberman, Rottweiler, Akita, Pit Bull and now because the Pit Bull is a banned breed the Staffordshire Bull Terrier and other larger Bull breeds are flavour of the month.

As with the German Shepherd the above mentioned breeds are caught up in a world of parallel breeders and owners. On one side we have the responsible owner and on the other...

Where the responsible owner suffers is in the stereotyping of the breed. They may have owned a particular breed for years without any drama but now when they go out many ordinary members of the public assume that their dog is dangerous and understandably get concerned. As a result they give out the wrong signals which worries a normally mellow dog.

If the responsible owner comes across someone with 'Vacant' tatooed across their forehead with a status dog on the end of a chain that could safely moor the QE II, the potential for trouble is great. 'Mr Vacant' will see the opportunity to get a bit of excitement into his pointless existence and will try, and often succeeds in, starting a confrontation. Often the innocent dog and sometimes owner as well are badly injured while the offender and his dog disappear into the back streets to boast to, and be congratulated by, his equally moronic friends. A short time ago I met one of these charmers.

I was out walking Phoenix, my nine month old Labrador, while visiting a relative. We were in a dog walking area and as we rounded a bend there was, stood on the path, a large threatening looking male on his mobile phone. He was dressed in 'gangsta' style and had a large Akita X on a lead. The dog was muzzled but displayed no aggression to either me or my dog. This seemed to displease this male who rattled and shook the lead in an effort to wind his dog up to show aggression. The dog didn't want to know: it wasn't in his character. On seeing that this male was seeking confrontation I walked around him only to have him move into my personal space so that our dogs would be within striking distance of one another. Both Phoenix and his dog ignored each other and we continued a short distance to our destination. Shortly thereafter as we returned, we saw this male tapping his dog around the head in the manner of a boxing manager trying to psyche up one of his fighters. The prospects for this poor dog are fairly grim. If the owner manages to turn the dog into the fighting machine that he obviously so desperately wants - which will give him 'street cred' and gain him 'respect' - then the probability is that the dog will be destroyed as a dangerous dog. If however the dog maintains its mellow outlook the owner will probably dump it like an unwanted toy. He will of course go straight out and get another unfortunate dog to bully.

Rescue centres across the UK are swamped with abandoned dogs, the vast majority of which are status dogs which have little or no chance of being rehomed and as a result many thousands are being euthanised. They have often been used for fighting and are no use anymore as money earners. Perhaps they weren't considered 'game' enough or perhaps the owner tried to bully the dog and it answered back. Whatever the cause the outlook is grim.

The real downside for responsible owners with the Status Dog issue is its unpredictability. Overnight anyone with a reasonably sized dog could find that their breed had come into fashion. These problems really erupted with the arrival of the Pit Bull in the UK. After some horrendous unprovoked attacks by this breed, some of which were fatal, the government stepped in and passed legislation banning the Pit Bull and several other breeds. The idea was that there would be no more imports, all breeding would stop and those animals already in the country would be subject to stringent conditions. As a result it was thought that over time the breed would die out.

The criminal fraternity however just carried on breeding in back street establishments and all their dogs overnight became 'Staffies' or 'Staffie/Pitbull' crosses. That lasted until they realised that no matter how small, any part Pit Bull made the whole animal Pit Bull and thus banned. Another quick play with words and now we have the 'Irish Staffie'. Most Pit Bulls are now bred in either Ireland or Finland although there's still a healthy breeding underground in the UK. As a result there the everpresent risk that as a result of a serious attack by a thug's dog there could be further legislation which could cause any or all breeds to be subject to huge restrictions. This won't affect the criminal of course - they'll just keep on doing what they want. It will only be the decent law abiding dog owner and their pets that will suffer. Be in no doubt that there is a huge anti-dog lobby out there and these people will seize any opportunity to make life difficult for owners and their dogs.

CHAPTER 11

Children and Dogs

Every child should have a pet, preferably a dog, but then we're biased. They teach children so many things, to care for another creature in an unselfish way, loyalty and even the facts of life, and death. All this helps to make a child able to better interact not only with animals but also with fellow humans and allows them to grow into a well balanced and caring adult.

If you decide to bring a dog into your household with your children it is important that both dog and children have guidelines. The dog hopefully will be brought up using PURE Dog Listening methods which will ensure that he behaves correctly, but it is advisable to teach the children how to interact with the new addition to the family before he arrives and gets swamped by over-excited playmates.

The following tips may prove useful and should be highlighted to children at home:

o Treat a dog as you would like to be treated - don't pull their ears or tails. Never shout at them: they won't forget how you treat them.

o Even if he looks kind, don't approach him. If he wants to come to you he will.

o Avoid things that might threaten the dog, for

example, backing it in a corner, running at it, shouting at it.

o Never look at the dog in the eyes - he may take it as an invitation to fight.

o Don't go near his tail, don't pull it or step on it. He uses it to express feelings.

o Don't disturb a dog when he's eating and never try to take his food away - he'll defend it instinctively.

o When you play with him don't pet him near his teeth. He likes catching things and it could be your fingers.

o Never try to separate fighting dogs, go and get help from an adult you know.

o Whether you are afraid or not, never run away from a dog as he'll take it as an invitation to chase you.

o You have two hands, he has only his teeth to hold on to you. Often you may think he wants to bite but he may only want to hold on to you.

o Only play with a dog when you are with an adult - dogs respect them more because they are larger.

o Never play tug-of-war.

o   No two dogs are the same: you have to get to know them. Treat them kindly and gently and gain their respect.

o   If you are expecting a few children into the house then put the dog in a safe place. If the children are getting over excited with the new addition, give them breathing space apart. Your four-legged friend will thank you for it!

Babies

We receive a large number of enquiries from concerned dog owners because they are either expecting or have just had a baby. Quite often a 'well meaning' friend will put the fear of God into the parents with tales of 'killer dogs' and they will be advised to re-home or even destroy their family dog. The dog will be jealous they are told. I used the term 'family dog' deliberately for that is what he is. Now, for 'family' read 'pack'. The pack must survive. The very fact of your pregnancy will enhance your status in your dog's eyes. As we discussed, as a general rule, only the Alphas breed. By you bringing a new member into the pack you are strengthening it and thus improving the survival prospects for all members. If you give your dog the right signals they will consider the new arrival a boost to the pack and a potential new friend. My wife and I brought up three children with trained police dogs in the house. I've still got the same number that I started out with and now have two grandchildren.

Give the right information to dog and child and

there will be no problem. The bond between children and dogs is wonderful to see.

Children and Dogs…No problem!

Let me tell you another story to illustrate how baby orientated a dog can be. My client was married to a member of the armed forces. She had suffered several miscarriages and had almost given up on ever being a mother. Her husband had been away for some time on active service and came home for a few days R&R. The day after her husband returned to his unit my client fed her dog and settled down in front of the TV. Her dog came into the lounge and regurgitated his meal in her lap. This lady was very switched on and the following day was at her doctors to announce that she was pregnant. When asked the usual questions about dates etc. she told the GP that her dog had told her by his actions the previous evening. You can just imagine the doctor inching away, keeping the desk between them and saying "Yes, I see. I'm just going to stand over here now." However, she was right and now has a very healthy boy. The amazing thing about this is that during the previous pregnancies their dog had never

186

exhibited this behaviour although the pregnancies had been confirmed and a due date given. Did the dog somehow know that these pregnancies were not viable? I don't know for certain, but canines will bring back food from the hunt and regurgitate it for a nursing mother. I like to think that the dog knew that my client was pregnant and wanted to stop her indulging in the dangerous pastime of hunting in Tescos by supplying her with food to maximise the survival of the baby.

So, you've got your new baby and you bring it home. There will be all sorts of excitement and strange new sights, sounds and smells for your dog to get used to. You will be exhausted and pleased to be home. Don't get into a situation where you are trying to get through the door with new baby and all the equipment that entails, as well as relatives, friends and neighbours all trying to welcome the new arrival, with a dog bouncing around trying to get noticed too.

Keep the dog in another room - a happy room such as where he normally sleeps or maybe the kitchen: most dogs like kitchens as it's the hub of the house and the food connection makes it a good place to be. A family member can go into the kitchen to make tea or coffee and interact with the dog as you do every other day when returning home. This shows that the status quo is unchanged: the pack still has credible leaders. It's vital that the dog doesn't feel isolated as he's done nothing wrong.

Everything is done on your terms, so in your own

time settle down comfortably with the baby so that you are relaxed and confident in your own comfort zone. Your other half can now bring your dog into the room on the lead without any stress being applied on dog or humans. Chat among yourselves - there may well be other people in the room - and make sure these people disregard the dog and only interact with one another. As always, keep calm, but if your dog is unsure of what is going on and therefore unsettled then remove him from the room without any drama. Allow him time to realise that everybody is relaxed and then bring him back into the room. This takes as long as it takes, proceeding at your own pace. The person holding the dog can then sit near the parent holding the baby and chat. Don't rush - we humans can become obsessed with schedules and timetables so that we can tick a box as 'job done'. Dogs don't have watches - to a dog the time is always 'now'. Because you are relaxed your dog will also feel at peace. When the dog decides to investigate the new arrival he will do this by both looking and sniffing. Keep calm and allow him to sniff around the feet but don't allow access to the head and face. At this early stage your baby probably won't appreciate a large wet tongue moving across their face!

All newborn animals are vulnerable and reliant on their parents for survival. Nature gives them a tool to ensure that mum and dad are kept aware of their existence. It is the cry, that ear-piercing head-splitting wail that says, "Give me attention..... ....NOW!" You, as the parent, have to interpret that sound and decide whether your child is hungry, in pain, needs a nappy change or just wants attention. This explosion of noise may well disturb your dog the first few times he hears it but if you deal with the baby calmly he will see that you have everything under control, that you are a strong credible leader. If you go into headless chicken mode you give a very different message to the dog i.e. that you can't cope. If you can't cope it means that your dog will have to, but he won't be able to cope either. A downward spiral...panic all round. Although you must remain calm, of course you must also remain vigilant so never leave a baby or young child alone with any dog.

Children sometimes are not taught that dogs, cats or indeed all animals are sentient beings and should be treated with respect. They are not there to be pulled around or ridden. Sadly some parents think it is something to boast about that their child 'can do anything' with the dog. Teach your child to respect all animals - it is your responsibility as parents and it will make your child a better human being too.

CHAPTER 12

New puppies

Choosing a puppy

Choose one that will fit into your house and lifestyle.

How lovely it is to have a new puppy - here is some advice to help you on your way.

o Buy from a reputable breeder who limit themselves in the number of breeds (and litters) they deal with.

o An advert where anymore than three breeds are listed as 'available' should ring alarm bells.

o Don't deal with anyone who only gives a mobile phone number as their contact details.

o Don't buy from a breeder who wants to deliver the puppy to you rather than ask you to collect. Some of these breeders will even want you to meet them in a motorway service area for the exchange. This is a real living feeling creature we are dealing with, not actors in a B movie spy story.

o Make sure the breeder will take back puppies for whatever reason at whatever age to re-home. These are the breeders who really care about the pups they produce.

o If you are buying a dog or puppy that is over six months of age, be careful. I have been called out to see people who have been sold a dog from a breeder which is six months of age and over and have been given various reasons why they are selling it on. Many times they find out the real reason 'why' when they get it home (within the first four weeks), by which time the breeder will not take it back. Aggressiveness with food or towards unfamiliar dogs, separation anxiety, chasing sheep etc. are fairly common issues that can arise. So, even if you ask all the right questions, take the dog out with the owner and see for yourself. And again, ask to sign a form to say you can return it for whatever reason and whatever the age.

o If you cannot see the mother then leave. If the mother or pups look unwell or under-nourished, leave. If at any stage you get a bad feeling about the place, leave. It is only this that will stop unscrupulous breeding. It is hard not to feel sorry for the pups and think 'I'll take one or two on just to get them out of there'. The kindest thing to do is to report the breeder to the kennel club and RSPCA. This is what is going to help stop puppy farming. Don't be duped by the breeder saying the bitch looks skinny because she is feeding lots of pups…she is simply not getting fed enough to keep up with demand.

o Some people find it hard to find the breed they really want and do resort to picking up a puppy they would otherwise not…use your head over your heart.

o You should not take a puppy away from its litter and mother before eight weeks of age. If the breeder is insisting then walk away. Between six and eight weeks they learn a huge amount from their littermates and mother: how hard to bite, what they can get away with and what not. They learn some manners from their mother and learn how to interact with their siblings which is a learning curve not to be missed. Miss this out and you may well be setting yourself up for trouble and end up owning a puppy with fewer skills in how to interact with its own kind.

Here are some other points to help you with your new arrival.

DO...

1) Buy a puppy from a reputable source.

2) Read the guidelines on the Kennel Club website.

3) Prepare all you will need for your puppy before it arrives: bowls, bed etc.

4) When your puppy arrives home for the first time, take it out so it can relieve itself.

5) Give it a meal, then leave it so it may investigate its new surroundings - a small area to begin with e.g. the kitchen.

6)   Be there with it, but put no pressure on it. Give it space and show your puppy right from the start that it is safe with you.

7)   Use PURE dog language from the very beginning to give your puppy confidence in your leadership abilities. PURE Dog Listening is not just designed to correct undesirable behaviour in adult dogs, it teaches all puppies and dogs how to fit in and respond to us. We use no gadgets or grumpy voices. This is a way to communicate on your dog's level so it truly understands what you are asking of it. Remember, you have taken your puppy away from a safe place with its siblings and mother, so you must make the transition as smooth as possible for it.

8)   Take it for a 'once over' to your vets at the end of the first week (if concerned, take it before) and discuss vaccinations and worming. Please read the section on 'Castration' in this book and do some research yourself - there is loads of information both for and against on various websites. Make an informed decision.

DON'T…

1)   Pick your puppy up if it looks ill, for example, with runny eyes, dry nose, runny nose, sore patches, fur missing, or signs of diarrhoea. Don't let your heart rule your head.

2)   Get all your friends and neighbours round to

cuddle and meet him - he needs to settle in and be comfortable in his new surroundings and family before meeting others.

3) Take him out for a walk in the big wide world immediately he has had his injections and let him run free - he'll get it all wrong, as a human toddler would if you didn't hold its hand.

4) Tell him off if he has an accident in the house - show him and reward him when he does it correctly in the garden.

5) Encourage rough games - he'll get it wrong. As he gets bigger it will get out of hand and accidents will happen.

6) Tell him how to behave. Show him and get him thinking of his own free will.

7) 'Sit', 'Stay' and 'Heel' are the icing on the cake!! It's how your puppy responds to you in daily life that is important. Does he jump up? Does he bite you? Does he hang on your clothes? Does he follow you constantly and seem unable to rest...? Show him how to respect you - the only way to do this is by using his own language, the only one he truly understands completely.

And remember there is no rush to bombard your puppy with information about the outside world. Let it find its feet at home and go out slowly but surely when the pup is comfortable with you.

What's in A Name?

Once you've got your puppy, you'll need a name for him or her. In fact you'll probably have one in mind before you even see the litter, so be prepared to find that your chosen name doesn't match up to the dog. You may have decided on Lucinda only to find that you have a Chardonnay at the end of the lead. Be aware that the name you choose can affect peoples' perception of your dog and by implication, their perception of you.

Parents often start their children off in life with a millstone around their necks by giving them some outrageous name which seemed very trendy and cutting edge when they chose it.

Dogs' names can cause other people to classify the dog, often unfairly, in the same way. If you pick Tyson, Killer, Crusher, Fang or Ronnie and Reggie then you are giving strangers the message that your dogs, and probably you, are aggressive. Once you give that message other dog owners will tense up, their dogs might become tense, body language signals will be exchanged and then it's game on. There's a major fight with injuries to maybe both dogs and humans. It's usually at this point that Crusher's owner says, "He's never done that before. He's a sweetheart at home."

When I choose a name for a dog I prefer a non human one, but that's just one of my little foibles. I have had dogs that have come to me at seven to twelve months already named (Ben, Jack) and it would have been confusing to them to change for no reason so they kept their original names. Keep the name to one or two syllables only - this makes it much crisper and clearer for the dog to recognise. Make sure that it is unlike any other family name. That could be awkward if you are trying to get your dog to toilet on command for example!

Let me tell you about Acco. He was my second operational Police dog and I was truly blessed with this animal. He was the perfect Police dog, brave as a lion, gentle as a lamb, with the bite of a crocodile. He could be taken anywhere and just knew how to act correctly in every situation. You may think that Acco is a funny name and indeed it is. It wasn't my first choice, but when I heard that I'd be getting a puppy from a very high quality German import stud dog I cast around for a suitable name. I didn't really want a human name nor did I want Fido or Lassie. Eventually the choice was between Ruff, short for Ruff Justice or Fudd because that's the sound a dog makes when it hits a suspect at speed. Neither of these names really did it for me. A breakthrough came when I was approached by a PC who had applied to join the Dog Section and was awaiting his interview. He wanted to know the sort of questions he was likely to be asked by the interviewing board. He then asked me who would be on the board and I told him that obviously the Inspector in charge of the Dog Section would be there along with a random Superintendent or Chief Superintendent and of course, ACCO. Like so many large organisations the

Police Service could not function without acronyms and ACCO is a case in point. With the exception of the Metropolitan and City of London forces every Police force is headed by a Chief Constable (CC) assisted by a Deputy Chief Constable (DCC) and several Assistant Chief Constables (ACC) and each of these ACCs has a specific responsibility which varies from force to force. It may be training, traffic, admin, or personnel but in every force the top ACC job is Assistant Chief Constable (Operations) or, ACCO. They are in charge of all real hands-on policing, major operations or incidents and all specialist departments such as Dogs, Marine Unit, Air Support Unit, Force Support Unit and CID.

As soon as I uttered the word ACCO I knew that I'd found the name that had eluded me. I visualised shouting out, "Acco, fetch" on training days. So when he arrived as an eight week old bundle of fluff he took on his real name. All was well until paperwork such as invoices for the vet's examination, innoculations and the like reached headquarters and middle management with no connection to the dog section saw the name. Panic set in.

"You can't call him that."
　　　"Why not?"
"Well, I mean, Acco."
　　　"Yes."
"Acco. You've called a dog Acco."
　　　"What's the problem?"
"What if *he* finds out?"
　　　"Who?"

"ACCO. What if he finds out you've called a dog after him?"

"He'll probably be flattered and he'll certainly find out because he gets monthly reports from the section."

With the support of my boss the name stayed and as we suspected, the human ACCO was happy with our choice and indeed took an interest in his namesake's exploits. It was not unusual for him to say to me when our paths crossed, "I see my alter ego had another good job the other night." It was of course gratifying for me to get the recognition of my dog's work but it was also, I believe, beneficial to the Dog Section as a whole as it kept us in the mind of senior management in a positive way. Several people held the rank during Acco's (the dog's) reign and were very happy about him until yet another post holder arrived. This officer had served most of his time in CID and made no secret of the fact that he had little time for anyone in uniform: apparently we were only issued a brain when we put a suit on. Now I don't know whether he didn't want to be confused with a dog or whether he just wanted to assert his CID background but he decided that his title would change to Assistant Chief Constable (Operations and Crime) or ACCOC. Maybe it was a Freudian slip - all I know is that I'd rather be called ACCO than ACCOC, although I've been called very much worse.

There were other consequences from having a strangely named dog. I was working an extended shift which was a normal day patrol followed by duty at an evening Aldershot Football match in company with Dave Ball, another dog handler. I was already cold and wet as a result of a search I'd been involved prior to the match and Acco was gloriously moist and muddy when a call came through deploying us to the Isle of Wight following a prison break. As we were sharing one van Dave had to drive me on blues and twos to Portsmouth Harbour to catch the hydrofoil to Ryde pier where transport had been arranged to pick me up. As I disembarked I saw a gleaming unmarked traffic car with an equally gleaming PC from Traffic Department standing next to it almost at attention. I approached him still soggy and with Acco only a little less muddy.

"Hello mate. Are you here to pick me up? "

"No. I don't know anything about you. I've got to pick up ACCO and his driver." (Don't you just love those moments when you realise what's happened?)

"I don't quite know how to break this to you but he (pointing to my dog) is Acco and I (pointing to myself) am his driver."

"What!?"

I repeated myself and he exploded.

"The *******s! They told me that ACCO and his driver were coming over and that he'd had a long hard day and might be in a bad mood and would 'bite my head off' if things weren't to his liking."

In honour of his anticipated passengers the traffic officer had cleaned the vehicle inside and out. He wanted to know where he could put a dog in a vehicle with velour seats that had just been thoroughly cleaned. By the time I'd explained that Acco wouldn't mind sitting on the nice soft seats I think the driver had lost the will to live. When I arrived at the divisional Headquarters for the island and contacted the Force Control Room at Winchester to confirm my arrival the staff there could hardly contain themselves.

"How did he take it when he realised that he was picking up a dog?"
    "Not very well. In fact extremely badly - he managed to drive the seven miles from Ryde to Newport swearing all the way hardly repeating himself at all."

All I could hear at the other end of the phone was hysterical laughter and the sound of people banging their hands on their desks as they tried to catch their breath.

When Acco retired his place was taken by Gaspode, named after a talking dog in 'Moving Pictures' and other books by Terry Pratchett. He was called Gas for short, a very apt name particularly when we were on nights. It's very hard to drive at speed to an incident at 03.00a.m. on a freezing January morning while trying to hang your head out of an open window to breathe.

Puppy Socialisation

Dogs and puppies do not become aggressive because they have not been in contact with other dogs. They become aggressive generally because they are dogs with the wrong idea about their status or they have been introduced to society under the wrong conditions, or perhaps have been put under too much pressure too soon to accept conditions that *we* perceive as non-threatening. Remember, aggression is not limited to dog-on-dog but can also relate to dog-on-human or dog-on-anything! These dogs do not have clear boundaries or a believable leader. We see the same behaviour in children where parents either have no interest in their child because it's too much trouble and would interfere with their lifestyle or, at the other end of the spectrum, we have the parent who treats their child as a Prince or Princess and panders to their every whim. In both cases it's not the child's fault but it makes it harder for them to interact with other members of society in a civilised manner.

We're not saying, "don't socialise your puppy," but do it in the right way: be choosy with its playmates. Work with puppies the same size as yours. If you have a Jack Russell then pick a Jack Russell size friend for it, not a socking great St Bernard. Let them play and work each other out, but if there is any sign of over-the-top play then just calm things down by holding them calmly for a minute or two, then release. If they play too roughly then accidents can happen.

Make sure the 'play space' is big enough so if one pup finds it too much it can get away and not feel penned in without any escape route. If it wants to hide, then let it. You can't force anyone to play, let them weigh up the situation and when the time is right they will. If there is a pup that goes over-the-top and is backing yours into a corner then the big bumptious one should be led away quietly. We don't 'do' bullies and he has to be shown that is unacceptable. Your pup will be delighted.

Introduce your puppy to new places and things gradually. Getting bombarded by too much too soon can make an anxious pup more anxious and a boisterous one more so. Slow but sure. There is no rush - take your time and the puppy will take things in calmly at your side with you taking decisions that make it trust you as a true and effective team leader.

The Benefits of Grooming

Grooming should be an at least twice weekly occurrence even if your dog has very short hair. It is a great way of spending prime relaxing time with him. Get the dog used to this at a very early age then it won't become an issue for you or the dog. With puppies, they will initially try and turn it into a game, so you must resist this as it will only make things difficult in the future.

Begin by using the back of the brush so they get used to the feel of something alien on them. If the puppy tries to bite it, take the brush away and make no eye contact with the pup. This shows it that you are not interested in a game at this point and all you want to do is get a job done – as time goes by the pup will enjoy this as some prime

relaxing time with you, as when you stroke your dog. It's great for his blood pressure and yours.
If you have a long or thick haired dog then the breeder should have given you advice on how to groom. If not, go to your local pooch parlour and ask them to teach you and watch them do it.

Apart from being a lovely thing to do, it gives you a great opportunity to feel any bumps or lumps your dog may have and be in a position to get them checked out at the first possible moment. It also makes them less resistant to your vet's examinations.

Did someone say, "Groom?"…Oh, yeah!!

A Remarkable Pair

There is nowt to dislike about puppies –
We all would agree this is true...
Except when they've dug all our plants up,
Or they try to dismantle a shoe.

At this point your smile may become rigid,
And your hands try to clench into fists,
You did not envisage this picture,
When you drew up your "Why to buy" lists.

You may become cross and disgruntled –
How could he do these things to you?
He really does not want to hurt you –
He's just doing what all puppies do!

Your puppy does not have agendas,
But his instinct will tell him to test,
He MUST choose a good and strong leader –
So you have to be "Best of the Best!"

So decide what you want from your puppy,
Then be steady, consistent and firm,
All young creatures are grateful for boundaries –
When they're shown them, it helps them to learn.

So give him the signals he yearns for –
Show him you are the leader to trust,
Then he will do all that you ask for –
His deep instincts will tell him he must!

And from there you will form a true friendship,
Born of mutual respect and deep care,
And you WILL be the envy of others –
For you'll be a remarkable pair!

By Leslie Harris

CHAPTER 13

Keep your dog happy and healthy

Vaccinations, Fleas and Worms

When should a puppy have it's initial injections? Every vet has their own ideas as to timing, so go along with your vet on this one - there is no 'right' or 'wrong' here, but it is most important that you do it.

There is a lot of discussion about the frequency of adult boosters. Here in England we give them annually. There is a school of thought that it is only necessary every 3 yrs, apart from Leptospirosis which should be given annually.

The best advice I have recently been given is by my vet and these are his suggestions:

o Leptospirosis booster should be given annually, it is a dead bacteria in the vaccination and is the only disease not spread from dog to dog - it is spread by rats and seeing that wherever you live you are never more than 30 feet from rats it is a very wise thing to cover for. This vaccine lasts in the body for up to 12 months and by 14 months they have very little resistance to the bacteria.

o The Distemper virus and Parvo-virus and Hepatitis diseases are spread dog to dog and a booster every 3 yrs is quite adequate, since a live attenuated vaccine is used.

o Vets are guided by the vaccine manufactures and the licence they give for the frequency of the vaccines.

o Worming and de-fleeing should be carried out every three months especially if you have children. Fleas are not so prevalent in the winter so just be vigilant. If your dog does ever have fleas be sure to treat the house too or they will re-infest quite readily and you can have a year round problem.

o If you intend to kennel your dogs at holiday time, you will also have to vaccinate against kennel cough. This is in droplet form given via the nasal cavity.

When I (Robin) was working as a Police Dog Handler, all our dogs got every jab going. Aside from our obvious desire to do the very best for our dogs in every way, we also knew we had to show that every care was taken with every animal's health because there is a virulent anti-Police lobby out there, very well organised and funded. They are constantly looking for ways to be offended and things to complain about. Racism, sexism, brutality, corruption, wearing the wrong colour socks (yes, really). Imagine their delight if they could find that Police Dogs were denied anything but the best veterinary care. What an emotive issue that would be. Some newspapers would make it a front page story for weeks on end. As a result we had to make sure we were squeaky clean. Our 'Force Vet' who was in private practice was very good and when our dogs came up to retirement age (at around 8 years) they would become the sole financial responsibility of the handler. He would give the dog a thorough check up and any problems found could be invoiced to the job rather than handler. If he felt a jab of any sort was needed he would give it. He rarely did as he explained that the dogs by the nature of their job were very fit. Any health problems were dealt with at once with no regard to cost. Because they worked in a variety of environments - towns, farms, factories and schools - they built up a resistance to most things. He used to say of our dogs that even their anti-bodies had muscles. Following the Doggie MOT he saw no reason to give boosters other than Leptospirosis again (except if kennelling). I followed his advice and all my dogs had long healthy retirements reaching at least fourteen and some fifteen years...not bad for a GSD or Lab.

I think that there is no doubt that most dogs are 'over jabbed' and others of course get no protection at all from their owners. This is one of those subjects that if you ask ten people you'll get eleven opinions and most will have a degree of validity. Why not do as I do: weigh up all the information and make a decision. As long as you're aware that lots of people will think that you're wrong whatever decision you come to then you can live with it.

Microchipping

By law you must have a disc on your dog's collar

with your address or phone number. Do not put your dog's name on it, your surname will do.

Micro chipping in this day and age is very important. Many dogs get stolen and lost every year. If your pet is lost and by some chance its collar falls off, then you will more likely be re-united with your dog if it has a microchip. My children know their name, address and phone number, unfortunately my dog doesn't and if he did he can't say it anyway and his written literary skills are pretty shoddy!!

Castration

There is a case to be made, in some instances, for castration. If you have both a dog and a bitch in your home, unless you intend to breed, you will either have to have at least one of them neutered or be very vigilant. If your vet advises you that your dog needs the procedure now to cure a medical problem, go ahead. If you do decide to go for the castration option we strongly urge you to delay this until the dog is at least 14 months old. When a dog goes through puberty it is not only testosterone that is pumped into the body but other vital chemicals which will be lost as a result of the procedure. These are all required for the growth and development of your dog into adulthood resulting in a healthy body and mind.

As humans we can tell by pain or changes in our bodies that things aren't right and can visit our doctor. Dogs can't do this: they are by nature stoical creatures and don't want to show signs of weakness. There is a train of thought that promotes keeping dogs entire until around age 6 and then, if there are no behavioural issues, considering castration to reduce the possibility of testicular cancer.

The usual advice given to deal with mounting behaviour and aggression is castration - supporters of this method never seem to have an answer if asked what should be cut off a bitch to improve her behaviour. As PURE Dog Listeners, we certainly know that it won't stop a dog mounting or biting. Let us be clear on this matter. Castration will not cure aggressive behavioural problems, in many cases it will not change anything and in others it makes them worse. Why not save your dog from a needless surgical procedure with all the attendant risks, and the resultant imbalance of testosterone in his body. Seek the advice of a PURE Dog Listener to help you modify your dog's behaviour.

If you're a man you'll know the answer to this next question - if you're a woman, ask your husband, partner or boyfriend whether he would be mellower and at peace with the world if you dragged him down to the local Health Centre one morning and had him 'modified'. Now let me think?

If considering the procedure research thoroughly and talk to your vet (because you will have chosen one you trust). Listen to his advice, weigh up the pros and cons and then make an informed decision.

Spaying

When considering spaying a bitch many of the same issues arise in deciding whether to say 'yes' or 'no'. There is the possibility of unwanted pregnancy, the considerable mess that bitches can make when in season which embarrasses some owners, not forgetting of course the legions of male admirers that will be banging on your front door 24 hours a day at these times. As with all dogs, the most important issue is disease prevention. It is wise if you are not going to breed to spay your bitch three months after her first season. If not done then it would be a good decision to have a bitch spayed once it reaches 6 years as they have a tendency to get Pyometra in later years. Dogs live longer in domestic circumstances than they would in the wild and throughout their lives they can collect benign cysts which later in life can become infected. If Pyometra results it is generally too late to save them as blood poisoning sets in.

As with all health concerns, know your dog, watch your dog. Are they drinking more or less than usual? Are they in pain or discomfort? Are their feeding or toilet behaviours different? If at all concerned contact your vet with as much information as you can. Listen to your vet and make a decision.

Choosing a Vet

You should take as much care choosing a vet as you do a nursery or school for your children. The nearest one may not actually be the right one for you or your pet. Take into consideration factors such as:

1)   If there's an out-of-hours service and if it is covered or shared by another local practice.

2)   Does the practice deal with surgery or will you have to take your dog miles away to a different practice in an emergency? Time is crucial in some cases and you don't want to waste time going to one vet, then being referred on to another, if the problem needs surgery.

3)   Meet the vets and explore/establish a rapport.

4)   Do they give out a comprehensive pack about their practice and what they offer?

Pet Insurance

Is your dog insured? If the answer is 'no' you are most certainly not alone: 87% of the nation's animals are not covered by pet insurance. Bet that surprised you - it most certainly did me! I wasn't insured and found myself with a £4,000 vet's bill last summer!! So whereas I used to say, "oh I can't afford pet insurance," this has now translated into "I can't afford not to have pet insurance!!"

At the end of the day it is peace of mind that you can give your best mate everything he needs and not have to sweat every time you visit the vets. It is nothing short of a maze out there to find an insurance that suits you, your pet and your pocket, so here are some useful tips from my friendly vet on the matter:

1) One of the most important considerations to investigate is what will happen if your pet suffers long-term illness or a condition that needs long-term on-going treatment. After a year some insurance companies say, "that's enough, you can't claim anymore - we've paid up to your threshold!" And there are some that when you renew will not insure for the illness you need to be insured for. Many of the cheaper companies keep their prices down by regularly doing this. So check the small print not the small price only!!

2) There are some companies that will not insure a pet after a certain age or may increase the excess to unaffordable amounts.

3) Some have an 'Insurance for life' policy, which means they continue to pay out no matter what age or the total bill. These are certainly more expensive.

4) Remember an insurance company will not insure a pre-existing ailment and very few will take animals over the age of eight years.

5) Some policies cover vet's bills only. But what happens if your pet causes an accident? Third Party insurance is vital. You may already be covered via your house insurance, so check first.

6) Some companies will also cover for added extras such as referrals to Physiotherapists, Behaviourists etc., so it's important to note that one insurance policy will not suit everyone.

So, decide what level of cover you need and if you go for the cheaper option and it lets you down, be aware you will not be able to insure with another company for that condition. Pet insurance is a minefield...so do your homework and good luck!!

CHAPTER 14

To breed or not to breed...
That is the question

We have been asked this many times and always answer with a question, "Why do you want to do it?" and "Look into it very carefully before you go ahead."

In my opinion (and the Guide Dog Society have got this right) you should look to the personality of your dog or bitch before embarking on breeding as well as her physical health. An over anxious or aggressive parent will produce a higher percentage of pups that are similar in personality. There are so many problems out there with dogs nowadays and if only people who breed took personality more into consideration then we wouldn't have half the issues we do today. So many dogs are either re-homed or put to sleep for behavioural issues (which usually strike bigger and better at about 18 to 24 months, as they reach maturity.) Okay, most behavioural issues exist because there is a communication issue, but the tendency for extreme behaviours has to lie also with the breeding.

If you do breed then do expect some come-back and consider having to allocate time to people asking for advice later on down the line...can you give this?

Firstly, it is a myth that it calms a bitch down. Some may, but it is not a guarantee. I've known bitches that have become aggressive through bad management by the breeder. Some bitches take the idea that because they have bred, it puts them higher up in the pecking order and they can become a problem thereafter.

Secondly, breeding is not a quick fix to pay off the bills! Sometimes a bitch will only have a couple of puppies, and if she needs a Cesarean that's the price of one pup out the window, and setting up to have pups with the right equipment is an expense in itself. The bitch will require double the amount of food during pregnancy and even triple her usual amount after whelping. Vet checks, vitamins and extra calcium all mount up.

It is hard work if you do it properly and then there is no guarantee that you will sell them all, so be prepared you may have to hold on to one or two.

You should also be in the position to take puppies back for whatever reason and at whatever age and either keep or be able to re-home puppies yourself.

I reckon it costs the price of three pups to have and rear a litter, maybe more if there are complications. The biggie for me was always interviewing potential owners. I have turned a few away just on the phone. The main reason is if the partner is pregnant or they have a babe in arms. It's a big thing having a baby and just as exhausting having a puppy - we are not wonder women!! So give yourself a break, get one sorted before you embark on the next - you want it to work, so give yourself the best chance possible.

I'm being a bit of a killjoy here, I know, but if you do decide to go ahead make sure you have the room, the time and the back up. It is great fun to have lots of little bundles at home, but there is far more to it than that.

So the choice is yours, do some research and go in with your eyes open.

CHAPTER 15

When your best mate goes to
the Great Kennel in the sky

It is indeed a very sad time and nothing can prepare you for it either. You must do what is right for your dog. We sometimes have to make that awful decision to put our friend to sleep, wow...that's distressing and extremely hard. But hold in your mind and your heart that that was the kindest thing to do, ending the unbearable suffering.

If you have a couple of dogs then you have to remain strong and not dissolve in front of the one left behind, you have to show them that in spite of your great loss you can cope and be there for the remaining pack as protector and decision maker. Having said that, it is easy to fool a human saying "Oh, I'm fine," but you most certainly can't fool a dog that easily, if at all! This is a time when it would be a great idea to go back to basics with Priority Feeding for a week and make sure your canine talk is top notch. You'll need to reassure your friend left behind that all is well and you will survive without the other one. A 'Calm Hold' rather than a cuddle is spot on for your dear friend - it will help him know that all is well and that you remain a team.

When is it right to get another dog? To my mind, the sooner the better. But that is me. We are all different, but do remember it is better to wait for the right one than go out and panic buy or panic adopt from a rescue centre. However much you need to fill that gap, take some time to find your next best mate.

If you have followed all the advice in this book you should now have a great understanding of your dog. You will have given all the right signals and completed all the rituals to make this happen.

All that is left for you to do now is…
ENJOY YOUR DOG!

CHAPTER 16

Our Charity Work

Alongside our colleague PURE Dog Listeners, we feel that we should give something back to those dogs that have had less than perfect lives or those who help us humans when we are in need or in harm's way. PURE Dog Listeners are involved in a wide range of good causes, a few examples of which you will find below.

The Story Of Nowzad and PURE Dog Listening
The dog from Afghanistan

Nowzad is a very lucky dog. Lucky to be alive and doubly lucky to have made it to the UK. In Afghanistan dogs are not kept in family homes but roam the streets of towns and villages living on their wits. A favourite pastime of the locals is dog fighting. When such an event is organised the men go out and catch a dog often by use of wire nooses. They then meet at the pre-arranged venue with other villagers and their captured dogs. The dogs are forced to fight and if reluctant are beaten until they do. Once the evening's sport is finished the dogs are thrown out to fend for themselves until being recaptured for the next event. If a dog has floppy ears or long tail the human captor will hack them off so that its opponent in the ring can't hang on to them. Nowzad was such a dog caught up in an endless cycle of cruelty and abuse. One happy day a dog fight involving Nowzad was disrupted by a Royal

Marine patrol which included Sergeant Paul 'Penny' (Pen) Farthing who subsequently rescued Nowzad with the assistance of other members of his unit. They were very gentle with him, they fed him and showed no threat towards him. Consequently he began to trust them. A bond had been made and as a result this was not where 'Pen' could leave it - he moved heaven and earth to bring this boy home to the UK along with some others they had adopted along the way. A charity was set up using Nowzad as the face of the organisation to highlight the plight of all animals in Afghanistan. The aim is to provide veterinary care and change attitudes to animal welfare in that country.

When I read the story in the papers my immediate reaction was to contact 'Pen' to ask if I could be of help. He welcomed the offer with open arms. It was going to be a tough call to help these dogs to live a relaxed life having been so inhumanely treated by humans. They had been given very good reasons not to trust humans and although people in the UK meant well, if they followed their instincts and tried to make friends with these dogs by talking to them, trying to stroke them or any of the other ways you might use to pacify a human, it could end in disaster. This had to be done properly and this is why we stepped in. I called Robin to see if he was interested in taking a trip down to the west country with me to meet Nowzad, Tali, Pen and Lisa. Of course he jumped at the chance and within a week of our first contact with Pen, we were there ready and waiting to give it our all to help rehabilitate these poor dogs.

*Caroline and Nowzad honing
their PURE Dog Listening skills*

The Visit to Nowzad's Home

Thank goodness for satnav - after 3 hours travelling and the obligatory breakfast stop, we found our destination with ease. We were welcomed into their house. Firstly, we were guided towards his computer to see for ourselves what it was like to be in a war-zone and what the forces and these dogs face on a daily basis. This was a real eye opener and it was brought home to us exactly what this dog had been through and the mountain to be climbed with him. As with anyone we do not just go to see the one dog, we have to assess all of them and teach the owner how to become leader of the pack, not with one but with all. You can only be given full trust if you sing from the same song sheet with all. They had four dogs in all, each with various behavioural issues. Two dogs were born and bred in the UK, then there was Nowzad and the other Afghan rescue: Tali.

Nowzad's main issues were that he was aggressive towards non pack members whether they were human or dog. Females (the human kind) didn't seem to be an issue and as Pen said, no female would have ever been in contact with Nowzad in Afghanistan. This we explained meant the dog had no reason to fear them or be aggressive towards them either, given that he had not experienced anything negative from us females. It was decided that if anyone had contact with the dog then it would be me. Even Robin, dressed in a tweed twinset and pearls, wouldn't fit the bill. Mind you, what I would have given to see that!

Nowzad's main issue, as mentioned above, (understandably) was aggression and he would bark at nearly everything and mean it. He was frightened of big crowds, bangs and helicopters. He would pull big time on the lead and was not particularly good on the recall either. In the house he would not relax and followed Pen and Lisa everywhere, scent marking in the house wherever he felt appropriate. It was also very difficult for them to have male visitors to the house as Nowzad would try and take a chunk out of them! The other thing that we noted was that he was very anxious with household appliances. He'd never seen any and wondered what on earth they were and if they were to be feared. Both he and Tali were so hung up on their past and the responsibilities of leadership that they were unable to play.

Pen and his wife Lisa were invited to Crufts along with their Afghan dogs Nowzad and Tali as nominees for the *Friends for Life* award. It is a big thing for any of the nominated dogs and owners, as none of them would have been to such a huge gathering before. The problem was that these two dogs were direct from a war zone and traumatised. If anything came into their personal space it would be considered a threat and would therefore be liable to be bitten. How would they handle the main ring at Crufts in front of thousands of people, applause and flashing lights, whilst in close proximity of other dogs and people?

Paul then hit us with the fact that it was only ten weeks until the big day. Just imagine a dog like

Nowzad entering the main arena with the crowds, loud noises and music: to him it would feel like the biggest fighting ring he'd ever been in. It was a tall order for such a disturbed dog to achieve in such a short time. We all had our work cut out and it was not a foregone conclusion that he'd manage it, or Tali either for that matter.

We took them through the five main areas of the method to gain ultimate trust - many behaviour issues are corrected by doing just that - but it also makes the more difficult ones infinitely easier to correct. Then we moved on to the other areas of concern. Nowzad's aggression was the big one for them and the general public alike: we had to get this dog looking to Pen and Lisa as the ultimate protectors inside and outside the home, and if anyone was allowed to do any munching and punching it was them, not the dogs! However we do not ask people to resort to that in order to get their dogs' belief and trust. The ultimate aim was to get Nowzad to trust them within the confines of the home first and tackle all the things that put him on guard there - once they had gone along this path then he could start venturing out into the big wide world where there were more potential threats and disasters awaiting. By doing the work at home initially, Nowzad and Tali were gaining a better understanding of them and their abilities as a convincing decision makers, this meant that the outside work became just a reminder of what had firstly been taught in an environment where there was less going on and therefore one that presented a greater ability to learn and concentrate. It is all in

228

the preparation. Pen knows this more than most having been serving in the forces out in Afghanistan - you do not go there unprepared without knowing how your team and leader operate. The same applies if you were deciding to climb Mount Everest: you wouldn't just gather a few friends together, take a couple of rucksacks and a bar of Kendal mint cake and walk skywards to the summit. Patience, preparation and making sure your kit is perfect, the team works well at every stage, checking and re-checking as you progress – it's a matter between life and death out there and that is also how a dog sees it...may sound dramatic but it's true.

Out and about we asked Pen to turn away at right angles from danger (showing you are neither a threat to the oncoming possible danger, nor prey) with Nowzad and walk back to the safe house (home) and by doing this the dog began to develop increased trust. Rather than walking towards danger and hoping that all will be well, by turning away, the eye contact is broken between dogs and also the human approaching. So in essence you are turning back to where you felt safe and where he felt safe with you. Great decision, or at least Nowzad thought so. As time went by Nowzad and Pen were able to increase the distance they moved from home and a simple direction change to the opposite side of the road in the future was enough. The local dog club had offered their services so that as we progressed we could incorporate parallel walking and cross packing in controlled environments. This was so important for the build up to Crufts.

If at any point Nowzad lunged or pulled on the lead then Pen and Lisa were taught to stop and turn away without a word, and when he was trotting by their sides to give him all the reward and contact as praise for choosing to follow (this meant that there would be no confusion for the dog). If you say something to a dog already doing the wrong thing, in this case lunging to fight, you are only encouraging it - you are rewarding his behaviour and he has your attention and back-up. Stopping him doing something with a grumpy voice and a tug results in a dog that will be stopped from doing the behaviour only because you hurt him or intimidated him, not because he trusted your decision. If a dog can create your movement then he is the decision maker and leader, so our focus here was on turning the tables.

With people entering the house, we suggested Nowzad, Tali and the other dogs were placed in a room away from the entrance door so that they didn't feel duty-bound to provide back-up and say who should and should not be allowed to enter. With visitors, the best way to show that you are not a threat to a dog is to give no eye contact and not to go and stroke the dog i.e. not to invade his space. When visitors were present we asked Pen to have Nowzad on a lead so if he tried to take a chunk out of someone's leg then they could swiftly, calmly and silently remove him to another room for 30 seconds of thinking time. Removed from the pack a dog will think: 'Oops, need to be with the pack, want to be with the pack, how do I stay with the pack? Ah ha - don't munch!'...light bulb moment. It is important to realise that this takes time and many short isolations to get through. This is better demonstrated to you by a professional PURE Dog Listener as we have to take a lot of variables into account and may have to make an adjustment or two to match our approach to your dog's personality and your house layout and family.

As far as marking in the house was concerned we advised that he should be on a lead initially when with them in the sitting room, so they could teach him to be calm in there and not get the opportunity to pace and mark, showing him again that it was not necessary. If there was an accident then it should be cleaned up with a biological washing agent to remove the fatty enzymes and so reduce the need to remark.

With the bang and loud noises which he would undoubtedly be exposed to at Crufts we taught him the 'Calm Hold' to reassure him in such instances.

When they then felt comfortable in all these areas, that was the time to take the offer of the dog club up, but to be sure that this wasn't carried out in a confined space.

Neither Nowzad nor Tali had ever played with humans and we also set out to teach Pen and Lisa great team building games to help then get the dogs to have fun playing in the garden and to help them maintain their dogs' physical fitness while they were on restricted lead walks.

They had a lot to achieve in a very short time span and they went to work on it. We made an arrangement for us to visit again three weeks prior to Crufts and in the meantime would keep in close contact via phone and e-mail to make sure all was going well and advise as necessary along the way.

Robin and I were there for six hours in total. It was very full on. Homeward bound and it was good to meet them all and we felt sure that they would put all the required effort in. They had to, they had a big date looming.

Robin takes up the story.

CRUFTS 2008 with 'The Friends for Life'

Nowzad and Tali were one of five nominees for the Kennel Club's 'Friends for Life' award which is awarded following a phone-in vote by viewers to the BBC's Crufts' programmes. The award ceremony is a huge event and can be overwhelming to both humans and dogs. It takes place in an arena in front of a crowd of 7,000 and is screened live around the world to countless millions. A daunting prospect for anyone but the other nominees included an autistic boy, an 11 year old girl with cerebral palsy (the eventual winner) who had been virtually confined to a wheelchair until her dog gave her the confidence to start walking. There were also two ladies with severe mobility problems whose dogs, one a Newfoundland the other a black German Shepherd had given them their lives back. Every one of the six dogs nominated would have been a worthy winner.

Caroline and I had gone to Crufts to support Pen and Lisa Farthing, not in a partisan way but to ensure that the dogs went into that arena in a calm state of mind - to do otherwise would not be right. Until the end of 2007 they had lived their lives in a war zone. Why should they trust a human unless he dressed as a Royal Marine? It was important that Pen and Lisa knew we were there: they knew what they had to do but they didn't want us with them every waking minute. We stressed to them the techniques that they had to work on right up to the big moment. It was important too that they knew if there was a problem at any time we were able to be with them within minutes to resolve the situation. We also had to be at the arena entrance to make that final decision at the very last moment, and wondered how the dogs were going to cope? Are there going to be both humans and dogs in the arena or only one or even no dogs, just Pen and Lisa? The Kennel Club passed that responsibility - to authorise Nowzad's entry to the arena - to us.

Because, as always, we have the interests of all dogs at heart we were, with the blessing of the Kennel Club, able to work with and offer assistance to all of the nominees and dogs. They were all delightful people with wonderfully supportive families. Obviously in a time-frame of a couple of days we couldn't deal with every problem in depth but that was not our aim. We just needed to ensure that both owner and dog were happy throughout the ceremony and not subjected to any undue stress.

It was my turn to drive and because I was having a lady passenger, the day before we travelled I washed my car and discovered that I owned a blue one. I then cleaned the interior and removed the old newspapers and cleared the pens (32 in number) from the front passenger seat and filled the fuel tank. I was leaving at 05.30a.m. and so wanted everything ready so that I could just get in and go. Just before going to bed I had to do a family pick up job - it was at this point that one of my headlights decided to pack up, obviously a taster of what was to come. To change a headlight on my car requires a degree in advanced electrical engineering and hands the size of a three year old. Late at night with an early start and long drive ahead the prospect filled me with dread. I knew that if I attempted it I'd be left with skinned knuckles and a foul temper. My wife then suggested I take her car as she wouldn't need a vehicle until daylight and could use mine. Problem solved, I transferred all my luggage, refuelled (again) and was ready to go.

The following morning I set off as planned, picked up Caroline en route and headed for Birmingham. We decided to go and locate our hotel first because as our decision to go to Crufts had been taken only in the previous few weeks all the hotels near the venue were booked solid. We managed to find accommodation at an establishment some distance away that was clearly modelled on Bate's Motel. Having found the place and so understanding why they had vacancies, we headed for the show.

If you have never been to the NEC at Birmingham

let me tell you that it is a very impressive range of halls. The car parks are massive and managed in a very unusual way. Normally the first arrivals at a venue are placed closest to the event, not at the NEC, where the first arrivals are placed in the car parks furthest away. When you realise that this could place you just a little bit north of Manchester you begin to sense the annoyance felt when you realise that the people who didn't get out of bed until after lunch are able to park by the front door.

We were placed in car park North 12. It was so far north that all the staff were Glaswegian! There are shuttle buses to the doors which are free after you've paid your £8.00 parking charge but the queues were horrendous so, having been told that it was only a ten minute walk we decided on that option. There is a different perception of time and distance in Birmingham but eventually, after coming across several remote South American tribes, we arrived at the doors only to discover that they were at the opposite end of the complex to the show itself but unfazed we pushed on.

Huge, crowded and noisy are the words to come to mind. When I was in Yellowstone Park, Montana, watching wolves, I saw reports of a prestigious dog show on American TV which was reported as 'The Worlds Biggest Dog Show'. They boasted of having 'over 2,000 dogs competing'. At Crufts I saw competitors wearing numbers well over 20,000. There is an array of halls used with breeds being judged for show, agility competitions and all manner of dog related activities. There were also countless stalls selling everything from really useful equipment to tasteless rubbish. For me the slate clocks with the naff pictures of various breeds of dogs on them got my 'Del Boy, Most Favourite Piece of Tat Award' although the reflective dog bandannas came a very close second.

Robin in the spotlight at Crufts

As previously mentioned the day progressed and Caroline and I developed a rapport with the Kennel Club staff dealing with the Friends for Life Awards, and got involved not only with Pen and Lisa but with the other nominees as well. We were heavily involved in the rehearsals which take place after the show closes to the public on Saturday evening. The

Kennel Club's instructions were that if we were in any doubt about a dog's ability to cope out in front of the audience then they didn't enter the arena. Even once they were in the arena we had to keep a close eye on their body language and be ready to remove them instantly if necessary. During rehearsals we liaised with the BBC crews who were incredibly helpful. Each nominee would walk into the arena when called and stand in a spot-lit circle. Once all five nominees were out they would be standing in an arc with not much space between them. At our request the production crew altered all the pre-set lighting to give a larger gap between dogs. This was done to take stress off of Nowzad and reduce the temptation to lunge and start a fight. At the conclusion of the rehearsal we'd done as much as we could not only with Pen but with the other nominees as well. We hoped we'd got through to Pen how important it was to do as we advised but Pen was a Sergeant in the Royal Marines, more used to giving orders than taking advice. We hoped he understood the potential for disaster if he got it wrong.

By the time we left to return to the car it was like a ghost town. All the Nominees, Kennel Club and BBC staff were staying at the Hilton Hotel directly opposite the NEC. We looked at the signposts and found ones that directed us to the South and East car parks but nothing else. I then found a sign mentioning North car park but it was preceded with the words 'No Access to'. We walked and walked until we found a security hut. When we asked for directions the guard was helpful but couldn't suppress a laugh. He pointed us in the 'right' direction...and off we went again. Two further encounters with security guards and over three quarters of an hour later we found my car, alone, in a vast empty carpark, no wonder it was whimpering. At last, back to the hotel and some food. Yeah right! We followed the directions to the exit only to find locked gates! We turned around and drove through the complex following various exit signs, all of which led to more locked gates. Suddenly there were no security guards to be found, they were all probably rolling around on the floor laughing, watching us on CCTV. Eventually, more by luck than judgement, we found the only unlocked exit from the site which for some reason did not have an exit sign.

On our return to our hotel we asked about getting a meal - no chance...it was Saturday night and they did have a large restaurant but they weren't able to do food, although they could sell us a packet of crisps in the bar. When we asked about other options we were given a choice between the Indian Restaurant across the other side of the dual carriageway and, oh I forgot, there was no other choice. We had a nice stroll to the eating place via the seductively lit urine-drenched underpass which although unpleasant did mask the smell of diesel.

On reaching the restaurant we were quite concerned - we were starving and it was Saturday night in Birmingham, the curry centre of the UK. Would they have a table for us? We were lucky, they did have a table for us, in fact they had all the tables for us. The place was empty, but no problem, that meant we'd get served quickly before the late night rush came in...wrong again. Still looking on the bright side, the wait must mean that our meal was being lovingly prepared, the herbs and spices being hand crafted by ancient 'spice gurus'. If you can't get a good curry in Birmingham then where can you? I don't know, I just know that you can't in this particular one. The meal, when it arrived, was simply awful. I've seen better looking fatal accidents and it tasted dreadful. The only saving grace was that the portions were small. When we left we were still the only customers...hmmmm, I wonder why?!

Sunday arrived, the big day, and we had an early start. We strode into the hotel carpark and I pressed the remote unlocking button on my car keys and nothing happened. After trying several more times I realised that the battery in the key must need replacing, strange as it was a fairly new car. After opening the car manually we found that it would not start. It was at this stage that I lost the will to live but, undeterred, I did a thorough in depth mechanical evaluation and discovered that someone (I have no idea who) had left the lights on all night. Luckily a good Samaritan came to our aid with a magic battery booster and all was well. Nobody ever need know unless my wife reads this book, Doh!!!

On our arrival at the NEC we found ourselves in car park North 10B, which seemed to be even further away than Saturdays North 12. At least we knew where we were going this time and were able to get straight to work. We spent the day moving between the NEC and Hilton Hotel, working with those nominees that wanted help or assistance of any sort as well as making sure that people were in the right place at the right time and in the right frame of mind.

When the big moment came all the dogs went into the arena and behaved beautifully. What a result - Nowzad was as cool as a cucumber. Just prior to their entrance Pen and Lisa were in the holding area doing some exercises with Nowzad and Tali, designed to focus the dogs' attention on them and disregard the noise and lights in the arena. At this stage some complete moron, a member of a 'Dog Training' club complete with heavily logo-ed polo-shirt tried to stare Nowzad out while saying to his companions, "He don't look that tough to me." A stupid move for anyone, but for a man who was so full of his own wind and importance about how 'good' he was with dogs, it was criminal. He took an aggressive stance like a nightclub doorman and kept moving so that he could maintain eye contact which as all real dog people know is a challenge when addressing a dog in that manner. Caroline told Pen to keep turning away from the threat and keep his pulse rate down so that Nowzad was not stressed. Both Caroline and I asked this man to desist but he ignored us - Pen was remarkably restrained, which was great, because had he reacted Nowzad would have lost the plot. I on the other hand was probably a bit more 'proactive' and had a full and frank exchange of opinions with this man which persuaded him that he might be better employed elsewhere. Anywhere.

Once the presentation was over we were ready for home. We even managed to get a shuttle bus to the carpark and find my car. Would it start? Yes!! We weren't even fazed when, as on the previous night, the gates had all been locked - we knew where to go. We arrived home very tired. It had been a hectic couple of days but we both felt that we had achieved something really worthwhile. There is no doubt that if Nowzad and Tali had gone into that arena without the groundwork that we'd done with them, or worse still, having had instruction from the 'Make them do it' Brigade, the evening would have ended in tears. Both dogs reacted in a positive manner because having been exposed to PURE Dog Listening, they understood that they were in no danger and therefore could rely on the human pack members to make the right decisions.

The Cinnamon Trust

The Cinnamon Trust is a wonderful organisation that assists elderly people with their pets in a variety of ways when conditions change or things just get too much. PURE Dog Listeners have been happy to assist this very worthwhile organisation on a number of occasions. My first contact with them was to assist with a client in a hospice suffering from aggressive face cancer. He knew that he was very close to death and his dying wish was to see his dog. This dog was big, grumpy and slightly arthritic. The patients wife had no transport and other family members were frightened to try to put a lead on him and get him in a vehicle. As a result I attended the home address and met the wife and dog who at first I thought was a large pit pony. After a bit of PURE Dog Listening the dog was in the back of my car and we were off to the hospice. It was incredibly moving to see the re-union of man and dog. Both knew they were saying goodbye but both seemed to be at peace. Very shortly after the visit the patient passed away. The dog seemed to reconcile with the change in the pack dynamic and became more mellow. A sad story but with the best achievable outcome.

Search Dogs

There are a number of groups of private dog owners across the UK who band together to train their pet dogs of all shapes and sizes as 'Search and Rescue' dogs. They offer to assist emergency services in any large scale searches such as missing persons particularly in large areas such as moors or woodlands. There are varying degrees of expertise in these groups. Some, such as the mountain rescue teams, are truly excellent and spend a huge amount of their time training in very realistic and often appalling conditions to improve on their already high standards. There are also dogs trained for use in specialities such as earthquake disaster areas where they are used to locate trapped people often under collapsed buildings. We have been working with some of these dogs in small groups or on a one-to-one basis to hone their skills in addition to their ongoing training with the group.

Rescue Centres and Breed Rescue Organisations

We and many other PURE Dog Listeners work with and offer support to rescue centres around the country as well as specific Breed Rescue organisations such as Labrador Rescue or Greyhound Rescue. This is a never ending job but hugely rewarding.

CHAPTER 17

How do you become a PURE Dog Listener at the PDL Academy?

Do you want to better understand and communicate with your dog effectively? Do you want to help other dog owners solve problems with their dog's behaviour? Would you like to work with dogs as a full time job? If the answer to these questions is 'yes', consider that all of these options and more are open to you if you decide to train to be a PURE Dog Listener. We provide the resources and the expert teaching. You provide the motivation and dedication and your dog will do the rest.

All the curriculum material has been written, prepared and will be presented by PURE Dog Listeners. They have worked with a huge number of dogs in a variety of situations for many years. The two founder members alone have over fifty years hands-on experience between them.

You choose how far you go in the world of PURE Dog Listening. Some students just want to have a better understanding and interaction with their family dog. Others, such as veterinary nurses, kennel staff or service dog handlers may want to add to existing skills. Any or all of these may want to become a PURE Dog Listener (PDL) and visit clients in their homes for consultations to deal with canine behavioural issues. There a number of steps along the way to becoming a PDL, but if you are motivated you can go as far as you want to achieve your personal targets. There are three courses. If you want to do consultations for clients you will need to complete both courses. If you are an interested dog owner and want information to apply at home with your own dogs then the first course might be sufficient for you. All successful students on each course receive a certificate.

Introductory Course

This level gives an understanding and overview of the techniques involved in canine communication with PURE Dog Listening.

This includes practical demonstrations, DVD footage with talks and discussions on all areas of canine communication.

In-depth Course

The course provides in-depth coverage of the method including problem solving and syndicate work.

If you qualify as a PURE Dog Listener do you have to work in that capacity full or part time? Well, you can do either depending on your own personal circumstances. Many PDLs start their business on a part-time basis while continuing on in their day job or while their children are in child care. Because you would be your own boss you can fit consultations around your own lifestyle. Maybe you only want to work in the evening or some weekends or it could be that working while the children are at school is right for you. Some build their business up slowly until they feel ready to go full time. Others find it a useful second income. Either way you will also find it very rewarding on a personal level.

Should you decide that the life of a PDL is your goal you will, on completion of your courses, have a great deal behind you:

1)   Comprehensive and ongoing training

2)   A tried and tested successful business format

3)   Ongoing advice and support including a free forum

4)   An immediate corporate image

5)   Collective promotion of the PDL brand, development and marketing power

It is hoped that students will meet up in the evenings to socialise and it is anticipated that at least one tutor would be present to interact with students in an informal manner and clarify any questions they may have. It is our intention to give you the ultimate learning experience in a friendly open environment. As one student said, "I never knew learning could be such fun."

Please look at www.puredoglisteners.com for more detailed information.

Authors' Note

As you will have seen while reading this book 'structured play' has a huge importance to all canines. It's an area that is often ignored in command training or misunderstood as it is approached from a human perspective. For this reason play is at the core of everything we do, whether it be teaching a dog manners or dealing with a behavioural problem.

It was during our research into training equipment and toys that we made contact with Ancol Pet Products Ltd., one of the UK's largest manufacturers/suppliers. We found that they alone, of all the companies we'd contacted, sold no cruel or aversive training equipment at all. They also shared our philosophy of ethical animal ownership and training and embraced the 'Leadership Through Play' element of PURE Dog Listening.

As a result you may well see a PURE Dog Listener's connection with Ancol, maybe on their display stands at pet shops or at shows in the form of advisory leaflets on a particular subject such as 'How to survive Christmas with a dog', or 'House moving with a dog'. You may well see us on their website answering questions from dog owners.

Our combined aim is to make life better for dogs and owners alike.